THE
SECRET
PRISON
GOVERNOR

THE
SECRET
PRISON
GOVERNOR

The Brutal Truth of Life Behind Bars

Anonymous

WELBECK

Published by Welbeck
An imprint of Welbeck Non-Fiction Limited,
part of Welbeck Publishing Group.
20 Mortimer Street,
London W1T 3JW

First published by Welbeck in 2022

A CIP catalogue record for this book is available from the British Library

ISBN
Paperback – 9781787395633
eBook – 9781787395640

Typeset by seagulls.net
Printed and bound in the UK

www.welbeckpublishing.com

To all the prison staff and inmates who've accompanied me on this journey, I owe you so much. You'll never be forgotten.

CONTENTS

PRISON GOVERNOR
A LEGAL DEFINITION

Pursuant to section 7(1) of the **Prison Act 1952**, *every prison* **must have a Governor** *– the person in charge of the prison* **is known as the Governing Governor**. *They're responsible for everything that happens within the precincts of their prison, from staff issues including training and discipline, to security and the overall care of inmates and staff.*

AUTHOR'S NOTE
WHAT LIES BENEATH

Many of the incidents described here are so personal and sensitive that I've had to disguise them to protect people and prisons from being identifiable. It's far better to reveal everything in a carefully structured format than to hide the truth away, and I want this book to help many people to understand how and why prisons exist.

You may on occasions have to suspend disbelief, though. I've had to find a balance between accurately reflecting the reality of life in prison and making sure I haven't given any legitimate secrets away. My publisher calls this process a 'narrative touch-up'. I've even avoided using real nicknames in case they offend those whom I've encountered over three decades in the prison service. Sometimes, I've also amalgamated characters in order to further protect their real identity.

The names of specific wings and prisons have been omitted for similar reasons. I've abbreviated the prison entry process in order to go straight inside the wings themselves, as that's where most of the action takes place. It's also helped me avoid all the seen-it-before clichés like strip searches and other standard prison fodder. I signed a confidentiality agreement when I joined the prison service, which I also could not ignore, so any resemblance to real people and situations in this book is entirely coincidental.

There is also little of the traditional prison slang here because it's not how I speak. I want my real voice to be heard, not a fake, streetwise version, which would not have been a fair reflection of who I am. I make no apologies for the language, though. Prisons are not politically correct environments. They contain brutality, bluntness and racism that is hard to match anywhere else on earth.

The ranks of officers in the UK prison service are constantly being chopped and changed by authorities, so I've tried to keep things simple by referring mainly to POs (prison officers) and senior wing officers to avoid confusion. Prison rules are also interchangeable and vary, depending on the era being referred to.

Then there is the vexing question of what prisoners should actually be called. Many outside the service claim that the word 'prisoner' is far preferable to 'inmate' but those inside prisons say there isn't much to choose between the two, so I've used both.

One piece of protocol inside UK prisons remains consistent, though. Inmates are not permitted to call officers by their names. They're encouraged to use old-fashioned terms like 'sir' and 'boss' when talking to staff. Since I didn't like these two terms, I ended up reluctantly agreeing to being called 'guv', although it felt almost as uncomfortable to me. It was only then I realised the motivation behind using these terms was to maintain a distance between us and the inmates.

Today I believe that attitude has caused more problems than anything else inside prisons. If I had it my way, all inmates would be able to call prison officers by their first name but that notion is still frowned upon, even to this day.

And finally, a few words of warning about this book. I'm not a professional writer. I tend to say what I feel and see. Sometimes it might seem a bit on the nose but that's what it's often like in prison. Staff and inmates cut straight to the chase, which is both the best and the worst thing about life in jail. I've got no doubt there'll be prison staff and inmates lining up to take a 'shot' at me for writing this book. I'll live with it because the truth can sometimes hurt.

INTRODUCTION
THE PRISON DETECTIVE

In some ways, I'm more like a detective than a prison officer because I've always tried to use my own thirst for knowledge to help solve problems and crimes that have happened inside jails over the past three decades. I think I first picked up this investigative instinct by reading Sherlock Holmes books when I was a kid. Holmes taught me to not look at things in purely black or white terms. I learned to examine the grey areas in the middle just like he did, because they often contain the answers in life.

This hopefully makes my take on prison life different from any previous memoirs. I'm also not obsessed with the clichéd brutality and supposedly dangerous aspects of life inside that are the main ingredients in so many prison books.

I've worked in prisons for more than 30 years. I went from leaving school with virtually no qualifications to running some of the UK's biggest and most troublesome prisons. My personality has evolved in many ways alongside my career trajectory inside the prison service. I started off young and naive and ended up as a governor with a paternal instinct and a single-minded determination to keep everyone in my prisons safe, and also to try to change the system for the better.

However, writing this book has forced me to re-examine my motivation in joining the prison service in the first place. Did I genuinely want to help the not so fortunate or was I more interested in the challenge of taking on some of society's most dangerous characters?

Throughout this journey, I've dealt with many seemingly insurmountable problems. These were situations and scenarios that were quite simply far beyond most people's comprehension. At the end of the day, I've always tried to show a more caring response to situations than many of my predecessors from the UK prison service's troubled past. I learned how to stop and consider situations, rather than run in with all guns blazing, metaphorically speaking of course.

No doubt this infuriated many traditional prison staff, but I've never wavered in my belief that patience and understanding must always take priority over punishment and retribution because what you see is not always what you get inside prisons. Also, throughout this same journey, I've often had to be a therapist and marriage guidance advisor as well as tackling sexual orientation issues with staff and inmates alike. Most people seemed to feel comfortable talking to me about it all. My other half says it's because they can tell I've been through a lot of the same shit as them (more on this later). I'm not sure that's true but what I have learned as a prison officer and governor is that you have to listen and you have to learn and you have to park your judgements on your doorstep every morning when you leave for work.

This is prison life from both sides of the fence. Some of it reads ugly, while other recollections retain a softer centre.

Either way, prison life has never stopped surprising me in good *and* bad ways. I'm not out to make a fortune from other people's despair, either. I'm hoping in some ways to provide a self-help book for law-abiding citizens who can't get their heads properly around the reality of our prison system. You see, locking criminals up and throwing away the key is definitely not the answer.

* * *

So what makes a good prison officer? If you've never been near a prison before (as a visitor or an inmate!), how could you possibly know? Being a 'people person' certainly helps. That doesn't necessarily mean you have to be outgoing or over-confident (I'm neither of those things). But you need to be able to interact with people, which means being reasonably articulate. The need to communicate under pressure is essential inside a prison.

The real-life dramas inside prisons come thick and fast. I've been called upon to save someone's life and prevent a threat to my own life all in the same day. It's just a matter of where and when.

So try and spare a thought or two for the 'screws' who've had to endure so much of this and consider these words that would have been on my tattoo, if I'd had one:

Be strong when you are weak
Be brave when you are scared
Be humble when you are victorious
Be badass every day

BEGINNINGS

I first became aware that there were good and bad people out there in the world when I was about four years old. Like so many children down the years, I was watching a Punch and Judy puppet show in a school hall with a bunch of other kids from my neighbourhood. When the policeman puppet came on the tiny stage, some of the kids next to me started booing. When he got smashed over the head with a baton wielded by Punch, they screamed with laughter. A child next to me elbowed me because I hadn't shouted encouragement to Punch to keep on hitting that policeman. Another child behind me pushed me out of the way because I was blocking his view. In the end, I turned away because I couldn't cope with watching that poor policeman getting a battering. My mum told me later that's when I burst into tears and she had to take me home before the show had finished. I tried to explain to her that it didn't seem fair the way Punch was hurting the policeman, but she didn't really get what I meant.

Around where we lived, the police were the enemy and you always stood up for petty criminals because they so often ended up getting a right-hander from the unfriendly coppers on the neighbourhood beat. A lot of my contemporaries on the council estate where I was brought up avoided me because I was seen as a strange, shy, loner-type kid.

I also had a posher voice than most of them because my mother had been obsessed with elocution and convinced me I'd have a better life with a superior accent. My father despised my mother's attitude as he was working class through and through. No wonder they ended up hating each other's guts. It was quite a relief when they eventually split up. I was just five years old but I noticed that the atmosphere at home improved the moment he'd gone.

Thinking back on it, though, I turned into an even more insular child after that, not helped by spending a lot of time in my bedroom with an assortment of toy cars and Action Man soldiers before burying my head in Sherlock Holmes novels. I did what so many only children of single parents do and learned to live a lot of the time inside my imagination. It seemed easier and safer than hanging out with the other kids in my neighbourhood.

But all that self-enforced isolation didn't exactly help my education. I preferred being at home to attending school and my mother was extremely easy-going, so bunking off classes soon became a regular habit. By the time I'd reached about 12 or 13, my father may have become nothing more than a distant memory but my education was not progressing in a very satis- factory manner. I didn't like most school subjects and, worse still, I hadn't got a clue what I actually wanted to do with my life.

Then when I was 14, one of my few friends was arrested for possession of marijuana and locked up in a youth detention centre. It seemed a bit over the top for just having some pot, but back in those days, any involvement with recreational drugs often led to a prison sentence, and so he went away.

A few weeks later I went to see him. Just getting in to see my friend on a visit seemed archaic. Everyone had to be strip-searched before going in and while that was humiliating enough for me, for women it looked downright nasty because the POs seemed to relish patting them up and down, and I saw far too much of that happening.

My friend was in a terrible state by the time I finally sat down to talk to him on that prison visit. He told me that older predatory males he was locked up with kept offering him cigarettes and food for sex and each time he refused, they'd beat him up even harder than the previous occasion. One six-foot-plus inmate had pledged to rape him in the showers 'within the next few days'. My friend was sobbing as he told me all this. So I promised I'd try to help him get a transfer to one of the smaller, more easy-going borstals on the south coast of England.

Over the following weeks, I barraged the prison service with telephone requests on behalf of my friend. I even gave an interview to a local newspaper about the appalling conditions inside that borstal. It must have worked in the end because he did eventually get transferred to one of those smaller youth prisons.

I came away from that experience wondering why most people cared so little about prison conditions and as that interest grew, I swapped Sherlock Holmes for grittier true crime books, which often centred on prisons. It seemed like a fascinating subterranean world and got me wondering even more about working inside the service.

Then I discovered that I could train to be a PO, despite my poor education. That was the real clincher for me. Sure, I'd have to start right at the bottom but at least it was a legitimate opening and the training didn't sound too challenging, either.

So aged 18, I took the plunge. Despite still being nervous and shy, I definitely felt a calling, as they say. But little did I know back then that it was going to be a long and winding road with lots of bumps and potholes all along the way.

PROLOGUE
FIRST DAY

Nothing can prepare you for the atmosphere when you enter a prison for the first time. Inmates stare at you. They smirk at you. Some even blow kisses. But you can't just stop and engage with them as you might do on the outside because of prison rules (but also because you wouldn't want to... basic common sense there). There's also the smell inside. It hits you the moment you walk into the main reception area of any prison. A toxic, nostril-stinging combination of bleach and sweat. While that is close, the reality is hard to describe in words.

I was bloody terrified on my first morning on the job. I could tell from the looks on everyone's faces that they all knew I was the 'new boots', as new prison staff tend to be called. Within minutes, I even found myself wondering whether I'd been wrong to want to go into the prison service in the first place. I'd sailed through the initial 10-week training course. Two officers told me I was one of the best teenaged 'apprentices' they'd ever come across, although I think they were most impressed by the fact I was a strapping six-feet-three-inches tall kid. And of course, no amount of training could replicate the *real* world of prisons.

But there was no turning back once I entered the jail that first morning. For when you're working inside a prison, the show must always go on. There is no other option. You can't just bring the curtains down and tell everyone to come back tomorrow. Less than half an hour into that first shift, one of my new colleagues told me to stop looking so wide-eyed as we walked along a corridor. I naively thought I'd actually managed to conquer my nerves by that time, but perhaps not.

"They'll spot you a mile off, son," the grizzly old PO barked at me. "Eyes down, chin up, shoulders straight and watch yer fuckin' back."

Numerous pairs of steely eyes were squinting at me through glass slits in the cell doors. No doubt they were all greatly enjoying my awkwardness. I knew it had to be like this whenever a 'new boots' turned up on a wing. But that didn't make it any easier for me to cope with.

I told myself to get a grip. There was absolutely no point in turning round and running out of the door. I hoped my deep, inner sense of nervousness would start to fade because I knew I needed to just get on with the job at hand. My stomach was still knotted, though, when an elderly inmate sweeping the floor near me said good morning. I was too shy to say anything back. That was my first big mistake.

"Charming," said the same inmate, who'd stopped, turned around and was glaring straight at me.

"Sorry," I said. "Good morning."

I was about to smile at him when I noticed my senior wing officer watching us, so I immediately looked down like he'd told me to. As I began walking down the corridor, I could sense the same elderly inmate behind me. Across the way, I was also aware that the senior PO was still watching us both. That's when I noticed him winking at the elderly inmate while they smiled at each other. It was only then that I realised they were both winding me up.

That should have pissed me off but I've never been the type to get antsy, so I brushed it off. In many ways I deserved it anyway. I think that attitude came from my childhood, when I felt obliged to grin and bear every glare and insult. Moments later, I felt a tap on my shoulder and swung around, about to reprimand that lippy old inmate. But it was the same wing PO. I didn't know what to say, so I waited for him to speak.

"Welcome to B Wing, son," he said. "You've just been mugged, mate. That old boy was testing you out. Never ignore them because they all want to take a chunk out of you."

Across the central area of the wing, I could see the same elderly inmate watching us with a wry smile on his face.

"Don't worry, son," added that PO. "He's one of the half-decent ones."

I was about to say something back when a cell alarm went off.

"Right. Off you go," said the wing PO nodding in the direction of the bell. "Good luck."

I knew which cell it was because a red light was flashing outside it, so I headed down the corridor towards it. I unlocked the cell and walked in to find an inmate sitting on the floor cross-legged with his back to the wall next to his bed. He just managed to lift his head up high enough to acknowledge my presence, while glancing at me with an empty expression.

He seemed as high as a kite but he wasn't being aggressive, so I stood over him and asked him why he'd pressed the alarm. He didn't respond and we both stood there in an awkward silence while his eyes rolled from side to side and his head kept slumping back on to his chest. I knew from my training that if an inmate was intoxicated it was often better not to ask them what they'd taken initially, as this might make them more agitated.

Then he started opening his mouth very slowly. I presumed he was about to speak, so I waited. But instead, he stuck his tongue out while looking straight at me and I saw there was a razor blade on it.

What the fuck do I do now? I thought to myself. Is he planning to harm himself or me?

I moved slowly back towards the door to test his responses. He didn't seem to notice what I was doing, so I quietly left the cell and locked it behind me. It was time to reassess the situation with colleagues now standing nearby in the corridor. As he hadn't assaulted me in any way, I presumed he'd been planning to take his own life but had changed his mind and pressed the emergency button instead.

One old PO once told me that up until the mid 1980s, most guards took the attitude that if an inmate was intent on committing suicide, he should be left alone to do it.

"We looked on it as one less piece of shit for us to deal with," that same officer told me. "There was none of this psychological bullshit back then. If they want to die, let 'em do it."

But my more recent training had made it clear it was my duty to immediately call in a prison 'Listener' under these types of circumstances. They're trained by the Samaritans to deal with potential suicides inside prison. However, the Listener couldn't be raised that morning, so my senior PO ordered me to return to the inmate's cell and try to keep him talking while we waited for the Listener to arrive.

The PO then explained to me that this particular inmate had arrived at the prison the previous evening. He'd been irritated because he was too late to get any dinner. He'd been further agitated by the plastic-sealed breakfast pack that had been dropped on the doorstep of his cell in the middle of the previous night. He complained bitterly to the early duty staff that it didn't look as if it had any substantial food in it. I had some sympathy with his complaints but wondered why this would make him decide to take his own life.

When I arrived back at the entrance to his cell, I hesitated for a moment. What if he attacked me? I noticed the same senior wing PO from earlier watching me, so I looked through the window slit in the door. All I could see were his legs in exactly the same position as when I'd left him earlier.

I took a deep breath and unlocked the door very slowly, listening out for any tell-tale noises from inside the cell. This time it was eerily quiet. He'd even switched off the radio he'd been playing when I went in earlier. As the door swung further open, I discovered why. He'd slashed his face, arms and chest with the razor blade while still sitting in exactly the same position as earlier. This time, he didn't even bother looking up as I walked in.

His head was slumped on his chest. I hit the emergency button before crouching down next to him in a huge pool of his sticky, congealed blood on the floor. That's when I recognised the death-mask expression. There was even a slight smile on his frozen lips. I started shaking uncontrollably and tears began rolling down my cheeks as the prison's four-man control and restraint team of POs surged into the cell.

One of them helped me to my feet before whispering in my ear: "Wipe the tears away, son," he said. "We don't want anyone seeing them in the corridor."

So I went into the cold autopilot mode of a prison officer in the space of just a few nanoseconds. That PO was right; extreme signs of emotion are not something you want to share with a wing full of hardened, manipulative criminals.

The same PO ordered me to go to the main wing office and wait for him there. I was in a daze. I suppose you could call it shock. My training should have prepared me for what had happened but it never fully does.

In the office, one of the duty POs – a middle-aged woman – made me a cup of tea. "There's nothing like a good cuppa after a swinger, darlin'," she said. That was the first time I'd heard the prison's common expression for suicide. It wouldn't be the last, though.

After I'd sat and sipped at that cup of sweet tea for at least five minutes, the senior wing PO came in the office and asked me if I was okay. I knew I'd have to write up a report at the end of the day, so I asked if he thought the inmate's death could have been avoided if I hadn't left him alone in his cell and gone for help.

"Don't beat yerself up about it, son," he said. "He made his decision. None of it's down to us."

I didn't nod in agreement because at that moment I felt entirely responsible for his death. And this was only the first morning of my career. By 9 a.m. I was back on the wing, standing next to the dead man's locked cell to ensure only the removal team were allowed to enter it and take his body away.

Luckily, none of the inmates knew much about the inmate because he'd arrived so late the previous evening that they'd all been locked up for the night. The senior wing PO didn't want his corpse removed until after the other inmates had grabbed their breakfast packs and been locked back in their cells.

The time passed very slowly as I stood there outside the cell door. A lot of stuff started going through my head about why that inmate had felt so desperate that he'd taken his own life. As I was running over everything in my mind, one senior PO appeared alongside me and asked: "Penny for your thoughts, son?" I had no doubt he already knew what I was thinking about.

But I didn't dare tell him what I really felt because that would have been seen as a clear sign of weakness, and that wouldn't do for the first day of my job. So instead, I managed a grimaced smile and just nodded.

That first morning taught me that violence and death were never far away inside a prison, so blaming myself for someone taking their own life wasn't going to make an ounce of difference. The initial shock wore off later that day and the brutality of the incident strangely made me feel more connected to my new career.

It was a harsh reminder for an idealistic 18-year-old kid that I'd just entered a world where sharpened pencils were deadly weapons and weak people were seen as expendable, legitimate targets for violence.

PART ONE

THE PRISON OFFICER

"The vilest deeds like poison weeds
Bloom well in prison air:
It is only what is good in Man
That wastes and withers there."

OSCAR WILDE

CHAPTER 1
DOG EAT DOG

One of the first lessons I learned as a rookie PO was to never say the first thing that came into my head when I was faced with a tricky situation. It was much better to take a deep breath and try to assess the situation in front of me. After all, I'd probably only get one chance to find a peaceful solution, and I needed to make that count.

Saving face is paramount as far as many inmates – and even some staff – are concerned. Once pride is dented, it's very hard to keep a lid on things. As a young prison officer, I tried to learn to put myself in the minds of the inmates in order to understand why certain things happened inside jail. That seemed to help me work out how to pre-empt some problems.

This process starts by appreciating an inmate's journey into prison in the first place. In most cases, they're brought to jail in a van straight from court after sentencing. That vehicle is known as the 'sweat box' for good reason because even in the winter months it's hot and sticky and smelly. It must be the ultimate wake-up call to anyone who hasn't considered their fate yet.

A lot of inmates I met when I worked as a custodial officer following my first stint as a wing PO told me that they were convinced the prison service deliberately didn't clean the interior of these vehicles because they wanted new inmates to suffer. I don't think that's true but I can't blame them for saying that, given the state of some of them.

As a custodial officer, I was responsible for handling inmates from the moment the sweat box arrived at the reception area after it had passed through the prison's sealed security system. The driver and prison staff would then complete their paperwork before inmates were allowed to disembark one by one into the reception area. There, I'd often supervise the prisoners being put into a holding cell. It contained other new inmates before staff, including me, began processing their entry into this harsh new world.

The first stage of this was to face a search which, these days, begins with the BOSS chair (Body Orifice Security Scanner) which an inmate sits on to detect any concealed metal objects in the body. However, BOSS is fairly limited in that it cannot detect drugs concealed in rubber or plastic wrapping. It also can't detect mobile phones. So a full strip search usually follows this, even in this so-called modern age when people's privacy is supposed to be top of everyone's list of priorities. This in itself is extremely stressful and can set a prisoner off on a path of violence from the outset.

Then follows at least one interview and assessment with a qualified professional to make sure they know what their rights are and to offer them counselling for physical or mental health issues. New inmates are told what courses they can do in prison, as well as getting a prisoner number and having their property itemised before it's locked away until they're released. They are also given a security category based on the likelihood they might try to escape, as well as the chances they might harm other prisoners and staff.

Most of the inmates I've talked to down the years have told me that while strip searches and so much of this process is indeed archaic, it is all something that most offenders know comes with the territory. Many prisoners actually find it much harder to handle when they arrive on the wing itself following that induction process. That's when their dire predicament really hits them like a ton of bricks. They're shown to a small cell that they may well have to share with at least one other complete stranger.

Back when I started in prisons, there was a strict policy of ignoring requests from inmates to change cells because of problems with their cellmates and I have no doubt this is one of the main reasons why so many new inmates loathed those first few days on the wing. It took the service years to wake up to the fact that prison violence could be cut by at least a third if prisoners got on well with their cellmates. Today, compromises are made when it comes to prisoners sharing a cell, which has definitely contributed to helping improve the atmosphere inside most jails.

Back serving on a prison wing during my early days, I soon noticed that the staff and other inmates always made a point of closely examining every inch of a brand new prisoner. That means everything from their haircut to the type of trainers they wore, because even the smallest details reveal something about a person.

Yet the one thing few took much notice of was the often shocked expression on the face of that new inmate. But I suppose most inmates know only too well that a lot of new prisoners just want to bury their heads under the sheets of those bone-hard cell beds and never come out again.

I appreciated right from the beginning of my career how distraught most inmates must have felt as they entered the prison system. So it was only right to try and play it softly, softly for the first few hours whenever one arrived on my wing.

I also soon discovered it wouldn't be long before they'd have to deal with some bully pushing them up against the wall of the showers and demanding a French kiss while threatening them with a shank. One old lag – as they often call the older inmates – told me that at the start of his third prison sentence, he stopped cleaning his teeth because he reckoned it put off anyone trying it on with him. "Nobody wants to kiss you if you've got green teeth, guv," he said.

The majority of inmates have to learn very quickly how to survive in prison and, as a new PO, I needed to do the same. Listening and learning was vital from the get-go. I quickly found out that most inmates were even more nervous than me and, of course, no one who is inside a prison can feel totally safe *all* the time. That's why prisons can be such edgy places.

I knew that every time I passed an inmate in the corridor, they could shank me or at the very least spit on me. Usually, they just smiled, nodded hello and walked on. But it's the uncertainty that makes prison such a complete mind fuck.

* * *

The floors in most UK prisons are kept immaculately clean because inmates spend a lot of time with brooms and mops shuffling around the prison corridors. That may sound like an old-fashioned clichéd image, but it's still true to this day. Those utensils are actually vital props inside prison because while cleaning the floors, inmates can listen to others gossiping, observe the bad prisoners at play and even spot the ones preoccupied by anger or love.

In the first prison where I worked as a PO, one fellow officer paid an old pensioner inmate £1 a day to tell him everything he heard and observed while sweeping and mopping the floors. This old lag soon found out what drugs inmates were smuggling in and who was going to get a beating, all while he cleaned the floors. Every day just before lockdown, the officer who paid this inmate would enter his cell (which, luckily, he didn't share with anyone) and the inmate would debrief the officer about what had been happening out on the wing.

Inevitably, though, one sharp-eyed prisoner eventually worked out what that old inmate was up to and confronted him. But the older guy convinced the inmate he'd been deliberately 'helping' that officer in order to send him off on a load of false leads, which meant inmates could actually conduct their everyday activities, including drug dealing, without interruption. The suspicious inmate reluctantly accepted the

old lag's excuse and left him to continue cleaning the corridors on the wing. No one would have known if he'd been
telling the truth about his double dealing.

One day, the officer who'd been 'running' the old inmate
was given a transfer to another prison. But before the officer
left, he organised a raid on the main drug dealers on the
wing, using information provided to him by his informant.
Typically, this officer hadn't given a moment's consideration
to his informer inmate's safety once he'd departed, and the
inmate who'd been so suspicious of that old lag in the first
place quickly worked out he'd been right after all.

A couple of days after that PO left the prison, the old
inmate was found sprawled out on the floor of the shower
room with his wrists tied together and the handle of his own
broom pushed up his rectum. He made a complaint against
the officer who'd used him as an informant but that was
thrown out because of a lack of evidence from any independ-
ent witnesses.

After recovering in the prison infirmary, the inmate was
immediately put in the seg wing for his own protection and
eventually transferred to another prison on the other side of
the country. I later heard that the same old inmate was so
terrified he'd be exposed at his new prison as a snitch that he
convinced the governor to put him in the seg unit for the rest
of his sentence.

The prison system can work to the detriment of the
inmates, and this was a perfect example. Prison justice back in
those days meant the staff were virtually never in the wrong.

This attitude ate away at me during my early days as a PO. I promised myself that one day I'd do something to try and ensure inmates felt less victimised. Once that was achieved, I felt, jails might start to become safer places.

CHAPTER 2
THE PRISON SINGER

Prison inmates and staff often take on a different persona once they're behind four walls – and that's not always such a bad thing, either. For sometimes unlikely, yet uplifting, things happen in prisons that take your breath away.

I was about two or three weeks into my second stint as a wing PO when I heard a man's voice singing the unmistakable words to Frank Sinatra's 'My Way' coming from somewhere along the wing corridor. Then an officer came around the corner towards me and I realised it was one of the oldest members of staff singing at the top of his voice. Moments later, he followed up with a full rendition of Johnny Cash's 'Folsom Prison Blues'.

I frequently tell people (because I'm immensely proud of the fact) that I once worked in a prison where an officer liked singing to the inmates. We'll call him 'The Prison Singer' in this story because he deserves such recognition. This particular PO was in his mid-fifties by the time I met him but you wouldn't think so from his refreshing attitude towards the job. He saw the prison service as a vocation, rather than simply a pay cheque, which he later told me had improved him as a human being. This inspired a lot of my own positive attitudes towards the job.

The Prison Singer taught me more about how to survive and thrive on a prison wing than any training manual or video. That first morning when I heard him singing his way down the corridor of the wing was also memorable because many of the inmates burst into spontaneous applause, with broad grins on their faces. Some even sang along with him. And not one of them mocked him or made signs behind his back, which perhaps was surprising.

I studied the Prison Singer's every move that morning. After he'd finished his improvised sing-song, he and other POs including me were due to herd the inmates into the exercise yard. I'd presumed that would be when he'd change into a more traditional, hard-faced PO. But that day he didn't need to because most inmates smiled and nodded at him when they passed him on their way into the yard. Then at lunchtime I sat down next to the Prison Singer in the staff canteen and asked him when he first began singing out loud to the inmates. He didn't answer me at first, so I repeated the question just in case he hadn't heard me.

"I don't wanna talk about it," said the Prison Singer, sounding more serious than when he was on the wing earlier. "I just like a sing-song. End of story, son."

I must have looked disappointed when he said that because after an awkward silence lasting a couple of minutes, he said: "It's no big deal. I do the same thing at home. It drives my wife and kids mad."

The Prison Singer went on: "You gotta try to bring a bit of happiness and hope into these fellows' lives. I've noticed the ones who sing along the most are the ones who keep out of bother most of the time."

"But weren't you worried that some inmates might use it against you?" I asked, nervously.

"Why would they do that, son? My shit singing is the least of their worries. If it makes 'em laugh, then I've done my job."

I worked with the Prison Singer for months and it was the same routine each time he was on duty. Every day he would sing, full volume, without fail. And he was one of the few POs I never once saw lay a finger on an inmate or even have a row with any of them. Make of that what you will.

When one old biker got parole after going up in front of the board 11 times previously, the Prison Singer sang him out of the reception area with his Frank Sinatra favourite 'My Way' as the inmate headed off towards the swing gates exit.

One morning a few months later, I noticed the Prison Singer looking uncharacteristically grim-faced as we changed into our uniforms in the locker room for the early shift. I didn't want to ask him what was wrong just in case he took it badly, so I said nothing. Ten minutes later, he was out on the corridor singing away as usual. The prisoners were as gracious as ever. One inmate even walked next to him for about 50 feet, singing along with him. The rest of that day on the wing went off quietly, as it so often did when the Prison Singer was on duty. He gave the impression he didn't have a care in the world. But I did notice a glassy, pensive expression on his face whenever he wasn't near any actual inmates.

Back in the locker room at the end of our shift that afternoon, he had that same grim look on his face again. He noticed me looking at him, so I smiled. He looked away. When I was in the staff car park getting on my motorbike ready to leave, the Prison Singer drove his car past me. We'd often shared a wave at this point over the previous months, although this time he didn't even look at me.

The next morning, I was the last PO to arrive at the prison for the early shift. There was no sign of the Prison Singer, which was unusual as he was always early for his shift. After another five minutes passed in the locker room, I asked one of the other officers where he was.

"He's retired, mate. Didn't want any send-offs. I promised not to tell anyone because it's his right to go any way he wants." The officer noticed the surprised expression on my face.

"He loved his job more than anyone I've come across in 30 years in the service," he explained. "He didn't want to retire but the rules said he had to go."

Once I'd thought it through properly, I realised it all made complete sense. He hadn't wanted to retire, so he acted as if he wasn't leaving right up to the end and that was why he hadn't waved goodbye in the car park.

Two or three months after his retirement, the same officer who'd told me the Prison Singer had retired arrived glum-faced for the early shift. He told me his wife had bumped into the Prison Singer's wife in the supermarket. "Poor bastard keeled over in a pub during a karaoke session. Apparently, he was dead before he hit the floor. Can you believe it?"

After the news of his death from a heart attack reached the main prison population, more than 30 wreaths and condolence cards were sent to the widow by inmates. She sent notes back via our governor at the time, thanking each and every prisoner.

Since then, I've done some research into the life expectancy of prison officers once they retire and studies have shown that the chances of them dying within two years of leaving the job are 60 per cent higher than for any other job, even including being a police officer. Maybe I've got that to look forward to.

RIP the Prison Singer. At least he went out singing.

CHAPTER 3
PAPERING OVER THE CRACKS

A lot of my fellow officers lulled me into believing I was good at my job from day one as a rookie PO by clapping me on the back constantly. They wouldn't have done so if they'd realised I was hiding a lot of my opinions about prison life, having quickly learned not to share them with most other officers in case I got into trouble for insubordination. I'm talking about everything from prisoner safety to the way that POs are trained to prioritise discipline and organisation over making individual decisions for themselves.

In my own case, it took one extraordinary, pivotal moment inside the prison service during those early days to push me into having the courage of my own convictions. It happened while I was in a corridor passing the time of day with a softly spoken middle-aged inmate, who'd always seemed a pretty decent fellow. He was about to go out to the exercise yard with all the other inmates on my wing. We were actually chatting about the previous day's football results when a large group of inmates surged past us in the corridor.

I noticed one inmate glaring straight at us both in an aggressive manner. As he moved towards us, I looked down and realised he was holding a toothbrush in his right hand. It had a razor blade attached to it. He swiped it across the side of the middle-aged inmate I'd just been speaking to. He doubled over instantly and collided with me as he fell to the floor.

I immediately crouched down to try and help him. Blood was seeping out of the corner of his mouth and he seemed to be staring helplessly up at me. I leaned across his body and hit the emergency button on the wall. The earlier crowd of inmates, including the attacker, had already moved on to the other end of the corridor towards the entrance to the yard. Not one of them looked back to see what had just happened.

Moments later, my CO and three other staff members turned up. The injured inmate didn't seem to be moving. I'd been incredibly naive and stopped to talk to that inmate in a notorious 'dead zone' uncovered by security cameras.

I'd seen who the attacker was but there was no evidence apart from my testimony that he'd done it. I'd been warned many times during training and then as a wing PO that my word would never be considered enough evidence to pursue a prosecution against an inmate. I also knew only too well that no other inmate would risk his own safety by informing on that attacker.

Within an hour of the stabbing, two senior POs questioned me quite aggressively in the wing governor's office. They couldn't understand why I'd defied express orders never to talk to inmates at that location because it was a blind spot with no camera coverage. As I tried to explain what had happened, I realised it must have appeared to them as if I'd allowed that inmate to be killed, which most certainly wasn't the case. Just like that suicide on my first day on the job, I began to believe it was all my fault.

Also, the guilt I felt about what had happened was making me react as if I were hiding something. The two senior POs grimly pointed out that I'd soon have to contend with rumours spreading round the prison that I'd been paid by one of the old-time gangsters on my wing to lure that inmate to his death. The victim had worked as a henchman for a drug baron and there'd been a lot of talk on the wing for weeks that he was an informant for the police, a 'supergrass'.

I wasn't exactly fighting my corner, either, because I felt so bad about what had happened. Both senior POs told me to stay in the wing office while they dialled in a prison investigative team to look into what had happened.

Everything after that felt like a blur. I can barely remember the questions those investigators fired at me but the whole process made me realise that a lot of the staff believed I'd been directly involved in the knifing. By the end of that day, I'd been warned by the deputy governor that I was suspected of setting up that inmate to be killed. I repeated yet again what happened and protested my innocence, but he and those two senior POs from earlier looked poker-faced as he told me I was suspended from work.

After that, I was escorted by the two POs to the staff locker rooms to pick up my personal belongings, most of which were in a backpack hanging in my locker. One of the POs asked me if I wanted them to call a cab because I might be in shock after what had happened. I refused and insisted on changing into my motorbike leathers so I could ride home myself. Later, one of my colleagues told me that my calmness further convinced some officers that I was guilty of involvement in the killing. They said I seemed so unflustered. In truth, I was terrified. I just didn't show it.

Then it all hit me like an Exocet missile as I drove my motorbike out on to the main road from the prison after my suspension. I suddenly had to swerve to avoid a car coming in the opposite direction and fell off my bike as it skidded along the tarmac. I was saved by my leathers and the bike wasn't damaged, but I was shaking like a leaf, so I pushed it into a nearby lay-by. I sat on a grass verge for at least 10 minutes trying to compose myself. Eventually, I noticed a red telephone box at the other end of the lay-by, stumbled up to it and called my wife.

Without telling her what had happened, I told her my bike had broken down and asked her to come and pick me up. But she must have known something was wrong from the shakiness in my voice. I didn't say a word on the 20-minute drive back to our house, even though she kept asking me what was wrong. Looking back on it, I should have said something but I was afraid if I did, I might implicate her in what had happened.

She cooked me supper that evening but I couldn't eat a thing. Then I sat in front of the TV like a zombie, still in my motorbike leathers, unable to utter a word. I could feel my wife watching me from the counter between the kitchen and the lounge area, so I carefully avoided any eye contact. When the telephone started ringing, I didn't move. After my wife picked up the receiver, I stood up without saying a word and headed towards the stairs.

She looked at me as I passed her and I heard her saying on the phone: "Thanks for calling back. I'm really worried about him." I should have stopped and told her not to talk to anyone about me but I couldn't bring myself to even speak. Ten minutes later, my wife joined me in bed. I was lying on my side staring at the wall. I didn't even turn to look at her when she got in next to me.

"I know what's happened," she said. "You don't have to talk about it but I'm here if you need me."

I didn't respond, closed my eyes and decided to pretend I was asleep, although I'm sure she knew I wasn't. I lay there for hours with visions in my head of that middle-aged inmate being murdered flashing past me.

At 3.30 a.m., I woke up after finally falling asleep less than an hour earlier and for a few moments wondered if it had all been a bad dream. Then the reality of my situation dawned. I got out of bed very quietly, walked downstairs, poured myself a glass of water, sat down on the sofa and tried to get my head around what had happened to that inmate.

The only other witnesses were the prisoners in that crowd who swept past us in the corridor. None of them would agree to give evidence and identify the killer. It felt as if I was doomed. I sat on the sofa staring at the TV for hours, afraid to turn it on in case the murder was on the news.

The next thing I remember was someone touching my shoulder. I turned round and it was that same inmate pleading for my help. I woke up to find my wife standing over me.

"You've got a phone call, love," she said. I opened and shut my eyes to try and get some focus. She passed me the phone and I said "hello" into the receiver.

No one answered at first. I heard someone saying my name followed by: "You need to come in to see the governor." It sounded like my wing governor. My heart jumped. All I really wanted to do at that moment was run away, even though I'd done nothing wrong. My wife drove me to the prison and stayed in the car while I went in to face the music.

As I arrived in the reception area, the only PO to acknowledge me was the one who escorted me up to see the governor. It felt as if I'd already been found guilty. When we reached the governor's office, the other PO knocked on his door and we entered. I expected to find the governor with his deputy and a prison service official but he was on his own. He told me to take a seat and nodded at the PO to leave his office.

"That inmate's going to be fine and he insists you weren't involved," he explained. "Apparently he'd fallen out with the man who attacked him about a drug debt."

I thought I was hearing things at first. I'd presumed the inmate was dead. I hadn't even considered that he might have survived.

"Thank you," I replied, shaking while trying not to show it and not sure what else to say. I got up, shook the governor's hand and left his office.

The following day, I was back at work on the wing and no one even mentioned what had happened. It should have felt strange that I was expected to carry on work as normal but it was a relief that things had returned to the way they were.

Today, looking back, I realise I probably suffered some kind of post-traumatic stress after that inmate was knifed. But back then, mental health issues didn't get much of a mention. Instead, we were expected to grin and bear even the most horrendous events, such as the one I went through back then. Bottling up stress is never the answer. Ignoring trauma just makes things worse in the long term.

The most important lesson that I learned from that incident, though, was that, as a PO, when violence kicks off inside a prison, you've got nowhere to hide. Whatever's happening, you have to deal with it. You cannot turn your back on anyone or anything.

CHAPTER 4
AVOIDANCE

Since the late 1800s, the term 'fish' has often been used to describe inmates who've never been to prison before. It comes from the phrase 'fish out of water' because that's what they are when they arrive. These 'fish' are easily recognisable in prisons because they're the ones who look nervous and lost. And that naivety can often cost them dearly, if they don't quickly adapt to the rules of the prison jungle.

I happened to be passing through the reception area of a prison where I was working as a wing PO when I noticed one new fish inmate studying me very closely. That threw me because there was definitely something familiar about him, although I couldn't put my finger on who he was. It's an uncomfortable feeling when you know that an inmate has played a role in your life outside prison, particularly when you have no idea what that role was.

I felt quite unnerved, so I made a point of avoiding direct eye contact with him that first day in the reception area. The following day he arrived on my wing and I found myself studying him from a distance, though, so he wouldn't notice me looking at him. By the time I sat down for lunch in the staff canteen that day, I was so immersed in trying to work out who he was that two of my colleagues asked me what was wrong because I'd barely uttered a word to them throughout the meal.

On the way home that night, I drove through at least two sets of red lights on my motorbike because I was still consumed with trying to work out who he was. That evening my wife asked me what was wrong because I was so slow to respond whenever she spoke to me. I apologised and explained I'd had a hard day. But when she asked me what had happened, I avoided her again because it had finally dawned on me who that prisoner might be.

While my wife was glued to the TV watching a soap opera, I went into our loft and found a box containing the few remnants of my childhood. Inside it was a family photo album. At the beginning of it were a couple of smudgy sun-bleached Polaroid photos of a seaside holiday when I was about three years old. In one of them, I was sitting on the knee of an awkward-looking man who my mother had years later told me was my father. We shared some features such as a bulbous nose and thick, arched eyebrows but little else. Looking at the photo then, I realised this man, my father, was undoubtedly that inmate.

I spent a restless night at home thinking long and hard about what to do and every time my wife told me to get to sleep, I shut my eyes and pretended I was. But my mind was racing. How was I going to tell the prison that I'd discovered my own father was an inmate on my wing? I'd planned to soon start applying for a promotion inside the prison service. Would his incarceration have an impact on my chances of climbing the ladder?

For the following couple of weeks, I did absolutely nothing. I froze in a sense. On the few occasions I saw him on the wing, he didn't seem to acknowledge me. So I presumed he hadn't worked out our connection, which was a relief.

One night I got home from work and was relieved to realise that my wife and children were away at her family's home. I needed some time on my own to think things through. I picked up the phone and poured it all out to my mother. She sounded shocked at first but then her voice hardened up. "Just leave it, love," she muttered. "He walked out on us a long time ago. You don't want him back in your life, surely?"

She also warned me not to tell anyone at the prison who he was. She was right because if it got back to my bosses, then my job really might be in jeopardy. So each time I saw my father anywhere near me on the wing, my heart jumped and I headed in the opposite direction. But I was sure it would only be a matter of time before someone found out.

I also felt overwhelmingly guilty about not being honest with my own father, as well as the prison service. I hated myself for being such a coward. I was so distracted by it all that I started making mistakes at work. And each time I noticed him in the distance, it got worse. Back at home, my wife inevitably worked out I was hiding something and eventually confronted me. She thought I was having an affair and was relieved when I told her the truth. But she also got angry with me for not dealing with it, even though I tried to explain to her that I couldn't risk it all coming out. We argued a lot about it that first night I told her. Worse still, the following day I was hauled into the wing governor's office and asked to explain why I wasn't engaging with the other POs properly. I insisted everything was fine.

A few days later, I almost poured it all out during a pint in a local pub with two other wing POs, who were worried about me. One of them even asked me if I had cancer.

I felt bad about putting them through it but eventually managed to brush over it all by convincing them I was having a few problems in my marriage, which was actually half true anyway.

But my father's presence on my wing kept eating away at me. One time we came face to face with each other in the canteen. He was just a few feet in front of me before he turned and headed off in the opposite direction.

On my day off the following weekend, I woke up in the early hours of the morning and announced to my wife that I was going to tell everyone at work the truth about my father. She seemed relieved. That made it feel like the right decision. But during the drive to work the following morning, I must have changed my mind at least half a dozen times and I was so distracted I nearly hit a pedestrian on a zebra crossing.

The earlier feeling of relief about my plan had been replaced with dread about what was going to happen. In the locker rooms, I tried to smile and act normal with the other POs but it wasn't easy because I was so churned up inside. Out on the wing corridor a few minutes later, I slowed down as I passed my father's cell and contemplated whether I should tell him of my decision before seeing my wing governor.

I was just about to approach the doorway to his cell when another wing PO turned the corner and started coming towards me. So I straightened up and walked on along the corridor. An hour later, I helped supervise the wing roll call and was completely taken aback that my father was not present.

For a few moments, I wondered if something had happened to him. If he'd died, then I'd feel even worse for never having the courage to deal with him and the prison administration. When I asked the wing governor about him, he said in a matter-of-fact voice that my father had been transferred to another prison over the weekend. His new prison was closer to where his family lived, and he'd been given the transfer on compassionate grounds because his wife had cancer.

Two weeks later, a letter arrived from my father's wife at my home. She explained that he'd told her that he'd recognised me, but that he'd realised exposing our secret might destroy my career, so he'd ignored me, and he fully respected my reasons for not wanting to acknowledge him. I was blown away by the humility and sensitivity of the letter.

We eventually reconciled when I visited him in his new prison. He expressed great regret about walking out on my mother when I was a baby. I also went to see his wife to thank her for bringing us back together. She was bed-ridden by this time and the cancer was working its way through her quickly. My father informed me when she died and I insisted on attending her funeral. My father was there on day release and we hugged each other awkwardly at the church after the service.

True, he'd abandoned me and my mother all those years earlier. But on the other hand, he'd protected me by not revealing who he was inside prison and that had probably single-handedly salvaged my entire career. My father proved to me that mistakes from the past should not impact on the present or the future. I learned to rise above the seething hatred and bitterness that so often fuels the atmosphere inside prisons.

CHAPTER 5
THE ULTIMATE 'FISH'

It's no surprise that most 'fish' – with no experience of prison or the traditional underworld – struggle in prison. But one inmate I came across when I was a young wing PO told me with good reason he felt as if he'd entered hell on earth.

He was a middle-class computer programmer who'd killed a man with a baseball bat when he burgled his house. He claimed he thought the intruder was about to pull a gun on him. He'd been found guilty of manslaughter and sentenced to five years, despite a high-profile media campaign to have his conviction suspended because of the mitigating circumstances. He looked like a broken man as he shuffled into the prison with his allowable belongings in a small backpack one morning. Unfortunately, this outward appearance instantly marked him out for attention from certain officers and inmates.

On his first afternoon on my wing, he emerged from his cell and I watched as he narrowly avoided bumping into a younger prisoner in the corridor. This other inmate was a classic smackhead type, who'd been in and out of jail for a stream of petty crimes that revolved around his addiction to drugs. The younger inmate stopped and engaged him. I had no doubt he'd be explaining to the new fish that he had to pay a special 'tax' of £5 before he could return to his cell.

As I approached them both, the younger inmate turned and gave me a knowing look before strolling off in the opposite direction. The fish thanked me profusely for intervening. I advised him not to mention his actual offence to other inmates because many of them would be on the side of the burglar. He looked a bit blankly at me when I said that, so I spelt it out more clearly by warning him they might well target him once they knew who he was. He looked petrified but he needed to be made aware of the dangers that he'd face inside prison.

Despite my advice, it didn't take the other inmates long to work out what this prisoner had done anyway. The morning after, word went around about how this guy ended up here, and someone shoved a note under the door of his cell threating to kill him. He was terrified and asked me for protection but there was nothing I could do. I explained that death threats were two a penny inside men's prisons and not to take any notice of the note.

However, in the canteen later that same morning, a few of the younger inmates began muttering threats under their breath at him as they stood in line for food. In their minds, he'd 'murdered an innocent kid', while I felt he'd defended his family against that intruder. At lunchtime, I stood on duty near the new fish as he tried to convince a younger prisoner why the burglar he killed wasn't an innocent kid. The inmate warned him he was lucky no one had shanked him yet, before getting up and walking away in disgust.

Over the following couple of weeks, I regularly had to step in between that new fish and the mainly younger prisoners, who clearly had him in their sights. He didn't actually get beaten up, although it looked as if it was on the cards. So I informed my senior wing PO that I was worried about that new inmate's safety and suggested putting him in the seg unit for his own security. When I told him this, he looked very doubtful and pointed out it was already full anyway.

The seg unit is like a prison within a prison. It's usually located deep in the main body of a jail and known to most staff and inmates as the seg or the block. And it's where the most intense prison time is served, often with 24/7 lockdowns that involve complete solitary confinement.

Back on the wing, another PO and I warned all the hothead inmates who'd been circling the fish that we were watching them closely and to stay away from him. As a result, many more of the inmates on the wing began carefully avoiding him and he became even more isolated. But then a couple of the older inmates stepped in and made an effort to talk to the lone fish. From what we saw, they certainly seemed more sympathetic towards him, despite what he'd done to that burglar.

Out in the yard, those older prisoners would huddle around the new fish to provide him with a protective shield as the younger inmates glared in their direction. I didn't realise it at the time but later found out that he was having to pay the old inmates to do this. They even taught him how to keep his eyes to himself and how to walk in a more aggressive manner, so other inmates became more wary of him.

By the time a new batch of prisoners turned up at the end of that month, the fish seemed to have ridden out the storm, as the harassment against him had definitely died down. However, I noticed there was one older inmate among those newcomers who seemed intent on watching the fish's every move. The fish himself hadn't even noticed he was being watched, but a couple of other POs and I worked out something was up.

The newcomer didn't actually go near him, so there was little I could do apart from keep an eye on them. He was definitely fixated, though, and we wanted to know why. So I accessed the new inmate's name to see if they had any connection to each other. This new inmate had been arrested for car theft about two months after the fish had been jailed for killing the young intruder in his home. His file recorded that he'd given himself up to police after the stolen car he was driving was stopped on a motorway. There seemed to be no apparent connection between the two of them, so we were confused.

The following lunchtime, I was on canteen duty when the same new inmate sat down next to the fish and engaged him in conversation. They actually seemed to be getting on quite well. That afternoon, I bumped into the fish in a corridor near his cell and asked him what the new inmate had been talking to him about. He said: "Nothing," but looked very nervous.

The following morning, I asked him again. This time he got more agitated and said: "It's between me and him – no one else." He also told me to stop watching out for him, claiming he didn't need my help and he could look after himself.

I had no doubt the fish had been intimidated by the new inmate, but I still didn't know why. So I tracked down some old newspaper cuttings of his trial. Photos of the victim's parents outside court were published alongside a couple of the reports. It turned out the new inmate was the father of the victim, even though they had different surnames. He must have got himself sent to prison deliberately in order to get revenge on the man who killed his son.

I confronted the fish about the whole thing the following day. He completely denied knowing who the other inmate was and kept glancing hesitantly over my shoulder in the corridor as we spoke. Twenty yards away the father was leaning against a wall watching us. I waved the fish away. He looked terrified and shuffled back to his cell. When I tried to talk to the father of the dead burglar, he denied all connection to the case and accused me of bullying him.

Later the same day, I found out from one of the older inmates who'd been protecting the fish that the father of the dead burglar had tried to kill the fish with a shank the day after he arrived on the wing. The older inmates stepped in and prevented it happening but only on the proviso the fish agreed to pay the father 'compensation' of £5,000 a month for killing his son. The fish was warned that if he was ever late with a payment, his family would be killed.

The harsh thing is how the older inmates had brokered the deal. They effectively 'sold' the fish to the father of his victim on condition they were paid £1,000 a month out of that £5,000 for arranging the deal. In prison, everything can be turned into a business opportunity.

When I mentioned all this to my senior wing PO, he didn't even seem surprised but promised to talk to the fish himself to see if he should be transferred to another prison. The fish refused the transfer proposal. I knew it was because he was afraid that if he moved prisons then his family might be harmed. The fish even hired a lawyer to try and convince the prison service he should be allowed to complete his sentence on the same wing. He continued to deny he was in any danger.

In the end, the governor insisted the fish was transferred and he ended up in a prison 200 miles away. It was a much smaller jail and located a long distance from where the dead burglar and his family came from.

I never heard from that fish inmate again. The father stayed in the prison where I was working for another three months. I never confronted him about why he was in there in the first place. There was now no point because his intended target had moved elsewhere.

Many years later, I bumped into the fish who killed the burglar in a supermarket. He thanked me profusely for looking after him when he was inside and apologised for not telling me the truth about that other inmate.

I was intrigued about how his family were after he was transferred out of my prison. He said he'd continued paying the father of his victim £5,000 a month for another nine months, despite moving to another jail. He'd done it to protect his family. It's a cruel business.

CHAPTER 6
UNDER THE KNEE

Racism in UK prisons continues to exist, even today. It's not an easy thing to admit but that's the reality of the situation. I was driven by a determination to try and stamp out this bigotry. But I had no idea what an uphill struggle it would turn out to be, partly because so much of it emanated from us, the guards.

This first hit me between the eyes a couple of years after I began as a PO. I was patrolling a corridor on the wing where I worked one morning when I noticed one of the senior officers standing outside an open cell door smacking his baton over and over again in the palm of his hand, while staring in at the occupant of that cell. I slowed down so I could keep an eye on him. I didn't know what he was actually doing but it was hard to deny that something was happening.

Moments later, a Black inmate walked out of the cell, ignored the officer and brushed past him. The same officer then yelled at the inmate: "You fuckin' rude black bastard." The inmate continued walking up the corridor without responding. The officer shouted the exact same remark at him again. This time the inmate stopped, took a deep breath and stood still. But he didn't turn round to face the PO.

I stepped back into a doorway to try and ensure the PO didn't notice me and I could continue watching them. The PO marched up to the Black inmate, grabbed his arm and twisted it up behind his back. The prisoner said nothing and shut his eyes tight, as if he was trying to stop himself reacting.

The same officer yelled: "On the fuckin' floor, blacky. Now!"

When the inmate didn't respond immediately, the officer kicked one of his legs out from under him and he fell to the ground. The officer then crouched down and shoved one of his knees into his back so he couldn't move. The inmate turned his head to look up at him defiantly. The officer drew out his baton, held it with both hands and pulled it under the inmate's neck until he was struggling to breathe. He leaned in close to the inmate's face and looked him straight in the eye.

"You piece of black shit," muttered the officer, who then noticed me watching him. The officer smiled at me, as if I was in on a joke. It sent a chill up my spine.

"Up! Now!" yelled the officer, still looking across at me, like we were colluding in this together. The inmate watched me but said nothing. He had a defiant, steely expression on his face.

"You gotta problem, blacky?" said the PO.

"No, sir," replied the prisoner.

The officer pulled his baton under the inmate's neck with both hands even tighter, so it was almost choking him. The inmate later told me that same PO had attacked him at least half a dozen times before this incident. He said he was so used to it that he just went into a 'zone' as he called it. He tried never to say anything back to him because he knew that would provoke the officer to hurt him even more, so his resistance was doing nothing.

But while I wasn't in the same position, and did have some power, I was still only a young rookie. I wasn't sure what to do. Should I intervene? Or just ignore it all? The officer glanced across at me again and, realising I wasn't going anywhere, relaxed the choke hold. He screamed at the inmate that he matched the description – in other words he was Black – of someone seen by two witnesses shanking another inmate in the shower earlier that morning. The officer then yanked the inmate back on his feet, cuffed him, put his hand on the back of his neck to push his head down and began shoving him back towards his own cell.

After the PO had forced the Black inmate into his cell and out of my line of sight, I finally snapped out of my state of hesitancy and marched towards them to see what was happening. As I entered the cell, I found the officer pushing the inmate's head into the toilet bowl as he knelt in front of it. He was screaming at him. "You filthy piece of black shit. You need a proper clean, son."

The officer glared up at me as I stood watching.

"What the fuck are you doing in here?" he muttered, while still holding the prisoner down just above the water level in the toilet bowl.

"There's an urgent call for you in the wing office, sir," I muttered, almost apologetically. The officer pulled the inmate's head up, slapped him gently on both cheeks and told him to watch his behaviour in future. Then he got up and walked past me, out of the cell. The inmate remained on his knees in front of the toilet bowl, looking up at me with contempt in his eyes.

"Am I supposed to thank you?" he said.

I apologised and insisted I was not the same as that PO. He looked doubtfully at me but asked me not to mention the incident to anyone else because then all the other racist POs would attack him as well.

I've often pointed out to prison colleagues that there is no way we can stop racism between prisoners if we're racists ourselves. It's never an easy conversation, because no one likes to admit that there is a core of racism in most of us.

If that incident had occurred today, the officer would have been fired from the service and probably even charged. Despite that, racism is still out there in full force and incidents happen on a regular basis, whether it's among guards or inmates. A lot of it is sparked by insults thrown around in the wing corridor or out in the yard or in the canteen.

When I was a young wing PO, we as staff were expected to ignore racism between inmates most of the time. I was given the impression by many officers that it was a perfectly acceptable part of everyday prison 'banter'. These days, thankfully, it is considered a lot worse than that.

Back during those early days of my career, I'd kept my own feelings on the subject to myself but gradually I found it harder and harder to listen to the blatant racism used by so many inmates whenever they were out of their cells. When two gangs of Black and White inmates almost had a shiv fight with each other in the yard one morning, it really brought it all home to me and I promised myself I wouldn't ignore it any longer.

The following day, I encountered two White inmates racially abusing a Nigerian prisoner in a wing corridor during rec time. They were yelling ape noises at him and referring to him as 'fuckin' Idi' as in Idi Amin, the much-feared despot leader of Uganda in the 1970s. But they didn't stop their insults as I walked towards them in that corridor. And when I 'dared' to reprimand them, the Nigerian inmate tried to brush it all off by insisting to me the two White prisoners had been angry with him over a drug deal that went wrong. He seemed embarrassed and kept trying to assure me it was all his fault. Meanwhile, the two men kept staring right at the Nigerian. One of them even tried to humour me by saying the Black inmate was a 'typical n.....'

That was the last straw for me. I pulled both inmates aside and reprimanded them as we stood in the corridor, while the Nigerian scuttled off towards his cell. As he went past some other prisoners watching all this from nearby, they shouted more racist abuse at him. It was only later I realised that he didn't want to side with me in case any White prisoners came after him again.

After the Nigerian inmate had disappeared from sight, the remaining watching White inmates moved away, although one or two of them did stand at the end of the corridor keeping an eye on me and the two racist inmates, when I began escorting them back to their cell. One White prisoner stood nearby muttering at me that it was none of my business and those two racist inmates could say what they liked to any of the Black inmates. The two inmates I'd originally reprimanded even had the gall to then nod their heads in agreement before telling me they thought I'd 'been out of order'. I finally ordered the two racist inmates into their cells or I'd put them on a disciplinary charge. They spat on the floor in disgust.

That incident reinforced my conviction that racism in prison simply wasn't being properly dealt with. But I'd also been naive to expect victims to complain about racism being directed at them because that would cause them even more trouble with others in prison. And this is undoubtedly why racism remains a problem in prisons across the UK to this day.

CHAPTER 7
DOING THE OPPOSITE

By the time I was four or five years into my prison career, I'd developed a kind of inbuilt radar that enabled me to spot signs of trouble on the horizon before anything actually took place. It came in handy, but it didn't make life as a wing PO any easier.

I remember one time during morning nosh (food) noticing a team of half a dozen inmates deep in conversation at a table, clearly planning something. But I couldn't pull them aside for just talking to each other, although I knew something was afoot. I also happened to be the only officer present in the canteen. They seemed to be glancing across at me, which made me even more convinced something was about to happen. It was only then I realised they were looking at a gang rival standing at the counter just behind me.

Moments later, six of the men swarmed past me towards their target, confident I wouldn't be able to stop them. I froze for a few moments, unable to decide what to do. I was heavily outnumbered, but I remember noticing dozens of other inmates in the canteen watching me avidly to see how I was going to react. That helped me find the courage to snap into action. I pressed the emergency button on my walkie-talkie and waded in with my taser. I was one of only six officers in the entire prison who was actually trained to use a taser at that time. As I charged in, a lot of the inmates involved in the canteen attack were so surprised by the way I reacted that they stepped aside. Unfortunately, there remained a hard core of three or four prisoners who carried on beating up their target.

I was doing everything I could to try to contain them – pulling them off their target, threatening and even tasering one – when a squad of 10 operational support officers with shields and batons waded into the inmates. After the battle was all over and everyone had been locked up in their cells, my senior wing officer pulled me to one side with a knowing look on his face.

"Next time, son, go in much harder, then they'll never take the piss out of you again," he said.

He paused before adding, "Remember this motto son: 'Smack 'em up before they smack you down.'"

I nodded but inside I wasn't really that happy with his advice. Using violence to counter violence seemed like a recipe for disaster to me. It creates circles of fear and revenge inside prisons and that can only lead to more life-threatening incidents, such as the one that just took place. It would be a long time later in my prison career before I finally started to kick back against the harsh, old-school attitudes inside my profession.

* * *

A few weeks after breaking up that canteen attack, three of the same inmates I'd tasered encircled me in what I took to be a threatening manner in a corridor. I noticed the senior wing officer watching us from across the corridor. But he wasn't coming to my aide, despite clearly knowing what they were intending to do to me. So I disarmed the three inmates with a smile to try and take the heat out of the moment. They looked nervously across the corridor in the direction of the senior wing officer. His eyes narrowed as he looked back at them. I smiled again. They studied me closely for a few seconds and all grinned back at me before retreating. The officer looked infuriated.

One of those inmates later told me that they'd been wound up by my fellow officer. He'd informed them that I was planning to teach them all a lesson following the earlier attack. They'd been so thrown by my reaction to them that they immediately realised they'd been manipulated and abandoned their plan to attack me.

This felt like an important moment in my development as a prison officer because it showed me that certain other POs were as much of a danger as inmates. I didn't just have to watch my back when the prisoners were around. I needed to keep an eye on *everyone* in prison.

* * *

During my early years as a PO, I was constantly on the lookout for diversions that were meant to distract prison staff from other behaviour. You get a nose for them. Something would seem not right and you'd sense that there was a plan afoot but you couldn't work out what it might be. Sometimes it could be pretty basic. If two inmates were having sex in a cell, another inmate would get into a scuffle further up the corridor to try and deter anyone from going near them.

Another classic diversionary tactic was a full-on tear-up between inmates in the rec area for no apparent reason. I'd end up prising apart the bad guys while something else more serious was happening elsewhere on the wing, which they didn't want staff to know about. Being caught in a shitstorm is all part of the job when it comes to being a prison officer, but I guess the key is how you handle this sort of stuff. Some of us can absorb incredible pressure on a daily basis, while others fall apart the moment there's a flare-up. In a perfect world, those more sensitive souls wouldn't get through the recruitment system to become prison officers in the first place. But life's not as simple as that, is it?

During my early career as a PO, I came across a few inmates who thought I might be one of those officers worth trying to intimidate. One threatened to shank me because I insisted he wore a prison T-shirt at all times. But instead of running to my senior wing officer, which might have been a sign of weakness, I carefully took my time thinking through the next move.

Later that same day, I listened in the corridor as the prisoner who'd threatened me boasted loudly to a group of other inmates about how he'd just intimidated me. I could tell he wanted me to hear what he was saying and I was incensed, although that in itself annoyed me because I thought I'd learned to rise above that kind of shit. Just as I was stewing, an elderly inmate known as 'Bench' appeared alongside me nodding knowingly. He'd earned his nickname after spending every day of his 19 years in prison lifting weights on a bench.

We'd built up a half-decent rapport and I actually valued his opinion, especially when it came to the other inmates.

"Don't let him wind you up, guv," said Bench, glancing in the direction of that same inmate, who'd threatened me earlier. How could I even consider getting revenge on him? I was a prison officer, not a fucking criminal. Bench nodded at me before strolling off as if he knew exactly what I was thinking. He was one of the few inmates I encountered who never tried to turn our association into anything more than just that.

For the following few days, I often caught my tormentor trying to stare me down as he passed me in the corridor, but I refused to respond and it must have worked because, in the end, he completely gave up trying to intimidate me. I just wish everyone inside the prison service realised violence is never the solution.

CHAPTER 8
9/11

Prisons are melting pots crammed with people of all races and religions. This often makes them tinderboxes where one small disagreement can spark an explosion of anger and destruction. But there was one standout occasion which perfectly sums up the good, the bad and the ugly aspects of prison life all rolled into one.

Surprisingly few people ever ask me what it was like in prison on that day in September 2001 when America came under aerial attack from Al-Qaeda terrorists inspired by Osama bin Laden. Most of us in the outside world know precisely where we were when those passenger planes hit the World Trade Center on 9/11.

I'd just cleared the canteen of inmates after lunch and was herding them back towards the main recreation area in the centre of the wing when I saw three officers standing avidly watching the main TV in complete silence. I noticed the images on the screen of a plane swooping low over the New York skyline before smashing into the side of one of the Twin Towers. Alongside me, inmates stopped in their tracks. A couple of them swore under their breath along the lines of "what the fuck?" as they began crowding around the TV set alongside the POs.

There were soon so many inmates and staff members gathered around the screen I had to stand on the first step of the stairway next to the TV area to get a better view of what was happening. I noticed two Muslim inmates whispering into each other's ears as they watched the news footage. Nearby, a couple of old-school professional criminals in their fifties turned and glared at the Muslims, just as the second airliner flew straight into the other tower.

Many inmates went deathly silent at that moment. A few more of them also looked across at the two Muslim prisoners, who glanced away awkwardly. The two older criminals from a few moments earlier turned and began pushing their way through the crowd towards the Muslim inmates pointing fingers at them.

I stepped in between them and ordered the two to return to their cells. One of them wagged his finger at the Muslims and yelled: "We're coming to get you." Some inmates cheered but then three or four other Muslim prisoners appeared behind me on the staircase. They began doing V-signs at the main group watching the TV and shouting death to the Americans and Brits. Some of the older, more traditional White inmates screamed back racist insults at them, calling them 'fuckin' P***s'.

It felt like the whole tinderbox was about to ignite. As the Muslim prisoners got more heated and angry, a larger group of other inmates turned in their direction and began surging towards them. About a dozen prisoners reached the foot of the open-plan stairs that led up to the next floor of the wing where the Muslim inmates were glaring down at them as the large TV screen showed a continual loop of the moments the two planes hit the towers. I needed to get near enough to the TV set to switch it off but that would mean having to force my way through an aggressive crowd, which might have further provoked them.

Suddenly, some of the older inmates pushed their way through the other prisoners up on to the actual steps next to me, just below where the Muslim inmates stood defiantly looking down at them. Three other POs appeared alongside me in support and we drew our batons to prevent the other inmates from reaching the Muslim inmates just above us. Things were escalating.

All of a sudden six back-up officers in full riot gear appeared on the floor, followed moments later by a further back-up squad of ten more POs with helmets and shields bursting through the double doors at the far end of the recreation area. While I was glad to see them, I remained caught in the middle of at least two different groups of inmates in a stand-off with each other, and had to stay there until the 10-man back-up squad reached me.

The hit squad screamed orders at the inmates to stand down but were completely ignored at first. Two of the POs then lashed out at one aggressive inmate with their batons, drawing blood. All of them immediately backed away, and the situation felt a bit more under control. The inmates were ordered to stand three feet apart against the main wall behind the TV set, which was still rerunning the 9/11 attacks over and over again. Each inmate was eventually escorted individually back to their cells. It was the only way to effectively water down the tension and avoid any more clashes.

When they were all finally locked down, I went back to the TV set to switch it off just as fresh footage showed people jumping to their deaths from the side of the twin towers. I hesitated before flicking off the set. Inside their locked cells, some inmates began banging against their doors. I didn't know if it was because of the terror attacks or because they didn't like the enforced lockdown.

I heard some Muslim inmates cheering and taunting the other prisoners by talking about taking revenge in the name of their religion. Other inmates bellowed at them to shut up. It was the first time I fully appreciated that a lot of young Muslim criminals had been indoctrinated by the idea of jihad – holy war. And a surprising number of those we had locked away in our prison believed the murders of those thousands of innocent people on 9/11 were justified.

Naturally, the following hours remained extremely tense. Angry inmates on both sides of the religious divide continued shouting insults at each other through their cell doors. At just after 7 p.m. – about five hours after the attacks – I was called into the control room by my senior wing officer. The governor of the prison was there and he told us that British security service MI5 were about to arrive to interview four of our Muslim inmates who'd committed terror offences.

Those four inmates were discreetly removed one at a time from their cells by three guards and escorted down to the reception area in handcuffs and ankle restraints. Each inmate was cuffed to a desk in the reception area's four separate interview rooms to await the British intelligence officers.

Back on the wing, the other prisoners quickly worked out what was happening and began yelling death threats at the remaining Muslim inmates through their cell doors. The POs on the wing that evening were convinced that when the inmates' cells were unlocked the following morning, which couldn't really be avoided, there would be violent recriminations against the Muslims.

Some of the prison staff were also quite emotionally charged by what they'd seen on TV that day. They seemed to have lost a bit of perspective and were less worried about their professional obligations to keep staff and inmates secure. When I subtly asked whether the four Muslim inmates being interrogated would be returned to the wing, three of the POs said that, as far as they were concerned, they hoped the Muslims were shot in the head.

That evening, as I and other duty officers walked past the locked cells in the corridors, we found ourselves facing a barrage of questions about the four missing Muslim inmates. We ignored them all, but that didn't lessen their interest or make the atmosphere any less volatile. While we had turned the TVs off, some inmates continued listening to the 9/11 reports on their radios in their cells and updating their fellow prisoners by shouting messages across the corridors either through their locked doors or by banging and bellowing through the paper-thin cell walls.

Down in the reception area, the four Muslim inmates who'd been taken from their cells earlier were being transferred to police stations in the centre of London where they could be more easily protected (or interrogated) than in the prison. Those other Muslim inmates, though, remained on the wing. I was worried that the rec area might turn into a bloodbath the following morning, but many of my fellow staff members didn't seem to care.

Thankfully, at a specially held meeting in the main wing office that evening, the governor and his deputy ordered that all remaining Muslim inmates should be moved to the seg unit and locked down in single cells while a decision was made about what to do with them. As we escorted the Muslim prisoners out of their cells, though, everyone else worked out what was happening and the entire wing erupted in shouting and screaming.

They began smashing and kicking their cell doors. There was also the noise of furniture being broken and death threats were openly being shouted by numerous inmates from behind their cell doors. At one stage, it felt as if the whole building was reverberating to the noise. All the POs, including me, were ordered to remain locked down with those inmates on the wing for the entire duration of that 9/11 protest. It took some hours before it gradually dawned on the inmates that their protests were totally in vain and they began to tire.

By dawn, the wing had turned eerily silent, the exact opposite of a few hours earlier. I never saw the four Muslim prisoners sent to those London police stations again. One fellow PO at that prison later told me they'd all been sent to the US detention centre at Guantanamo Bay in Cuba, where so many terror suspects were taken and imprisoned without trial following 9/11.

The following morning, a lot of the inmates talked incessantly about the attacks between their locked cells. By mid-morning, we'd agreed to requests from inmates to turn the main TV set in the rec area back on. All the flaps to inmates' cell doors were left up so they could watch the TV screen from their cells. One inmate – who had relatives living in New York City – yelled out that he was worried about his family. I talked to him through his cell door and assured him that he'd be allowed to call his family later that day to check on their wellbeing.

Unfortunately, one senior staff member reported me to the governor for allowing the inmates to continue watching the 9/11 news coverage. That PO complained that my action could have incited further violence, which most certainly was not the case, or at least not the intention. However, when I was summoned to the governor's office the following day to explain myself, I got a surprise. He told me he considered the complaint to be baseless and congratulated me on my decision to turn the TV back on because he felt the inmates had a perfect right to watch it.

I never discovered the identity of the staff member who complained, but it was another timely reminder that it wasn't just the inmates who were watching my every move. Even more importantly, though, the entire law enforcement system in the UK and much of the rest of the world changed after 9/11. It felt at times as if the terrorists had us all under siege.

Practising, law-abiding Muslims found themselves the targets of an outrageous backlash. Inside prisons across the UK and many countries in the world, Muslim prisoners were placed in seg units, often for their own safety. Eventually, a lot of Muslim inmates in the UK were transferred to a brand-new, medium-to-high-security prison south of London as a direct response to the backlash against them. Others were spread out in a variety of prisons across the country. 9/11 was an unforgettable moment in my prison service career, as it was for many other officers. Those terror attacks led to a much more challenging and complex world, both outside and inside prison.

CHAPTER 9
THE UNMENTIONABLE

Making inmates feel bad about themselves can spark a combination of guilt and anger in them – and that can result in serious problems.

So, as a PO, I quickly learned not to judge anyone, especially when it came to the most sensitive subject of all – sex. TV and films often give the impression it is rampant inside all prisons. In the real world, the libido of most prisoners tends to fade once they're under lock and key. But there are a few who 'convert' their sexual preferences inside prison, although most would swear on a Bible (or whatever their religion might require) they were 100 per cent heterosexual.

One professional gangster explained it all to me like this: "Sex is a funny old business," he said. "You think you'd never go near a bloke, ever. But when you're inside and you feel the need... well... that's different, ain't it?" To him, inmates either put sex completely out of their minds or they let it burn a big hole in their brains. And sex is an escape from the day-to-day boredom of prison life, so really it fulfils two needs.

That gangster compared his need for sex to the 'hits' of excitement and risk that draw most professional villains into crime in the first place. "And the next thing you know you're gettin' a blow job," he added with a naughty twinkle in his eye. Sex perfectly sums up the way that people's attitudes and mentality changes once they're inside a prison.

Another professional criminal serving a long stretch in prison once told me: "Shagging inside is not the same as cheating on your missus. It just doesn't count. My old lady knows I sometimes need servicing. It's just a means to an end. I'd never admit it to anyone outside and she said she'll always keep it secret."

When I first started working as a wing officer more than 30 years ago, the AIDS epidemic was still around and very much widespread inside a lot of men's prisons in the UK. Tests were regularly carried out on openly gay inmates but few men had come out back then. Plus, the inmates who 'went gay' temporarily while serving prison sentences would never admit to having gay experiences, so the prison service didn't know who had AIDS because most candidates refused to even have an AIDS test. Some inmates even used the fear of AIDS as a chilling bargaining tool to blackmail prisoners afraid that their gay activities might be exposed.

Also, sex itself was – and still is – often used as a commodity inside prison. Some men 'serviced' other inmates in return for protection against attacks from others targeting them for being gay. Ironic. Others deliberately spread rumours about specific inmates having AIDS in order to prevent them selling their bodies because sex could be big business inside prisons.

When I was a wing PO at one of the UK's biggest prisons, two separate vice rings were run virtually under the nose of the authorities. Each operated like a brothel within the walls of the prison, with criminals pimping out other inmates for sex. Obviously, this was done discreetly because few prisoners wanted others to know they were sleeping with men. But their existence was well known on the jailhouse rumour mill. However, like so many competitive businesses inside prison, a war eventually broke out between the inmates running these jailhouse brothels when they began poaching each other's 'customers'.

The leader of one of the vice rings then began spreading rumours around the prison that one of the men from the other sex-for-sale operation had AIDS. The inmate target of these rumours was so outraged that he hired one of the prison's most dangerous inmates to kill the prisoner who was spreading these supposed lies. Fortunately, the hit was cancelled at the last moment when one of the prison's most astute gangsters got both sides to agree to amalgamate into one vice ring under his stewardship. He kept the peace (and also a 25 per cent commission).

* * *

Among the inmates at one prison where I worked, there were two popular ones known as Bill and Ben. They were both hardened ex-bank robbers in their late fifties who'd been professional criminals for most of their adult lives. They'd each been to prison at least three times before, although this time around they behaved like model prisoners and cellmates.

Bill and Ben had seen every side of prison life before and seemed to have reached a stage in their lives where serving their time and getting out on probation as quickly as possible was clearly their main priority. During the first couple of months, I was a PO at their prison and they seemed the perfect prisoners. They'd hang out in the yard together, settle in a corner, puff a few ciggies and usually wander back to their cell before most others had even left the yard. Most officers knew and liked them too.

Each of them had regular visits from their wives and grown-up kids and grandchildren once a month. Both men were regular snooker players and even belonged to a card school. Weirdly, though, at some point, over the course of a number of months, I noticed that they gradually started withdrawing from everyday prison activities.

Most officers were convinced this was a deliberate attempt by them to keep an even lower profile so they didn't get into any trouble, which might threaten their release dates. When one younger inmate pushed in front of Ben in a queue in the canteen, other prisoners and staff such as me were astonished that the older inmate didn't react, except to shrug his shoulders. One senior officer told me that in his heyday, Ben would have beaten that younger inmate to a pulp. But times had clearly changed.

A few days later, I was walking past Bill and Ben's cell when I heard someone crying. When I looked in, Ben was lying red-faced on his own on the top bunk, while Bill seemed to be reading a book on the bed below him. Neither of them said a word when I looked in. It was obvious something was going on, although I couldn't put my finger on exactly what it was, so I just nodded at both of them and left their cell.

That lunchtime I mentioned Bill and Ben to an older PO, who immediately said I should stop fretting about them. He said they were probably testing me to see how I reacted to them. The senior PO didn't properly expand on what exactly he meant, except to shrug his shoulders and dive back into his steak and kidney pie.

A few days later, Bill and Ben engaged me in some polite conversation in the yard about the weather and politics. Bill even said to me at the end: "You're a good bloke, guv. Wish there were more like you in this place."

The following day, they didn't come out of their cell for rec time, so I went to see why they hadn't appeared. As I stood at the cell door, Bill looked across at Ben awkwardly and they exchanged furtive glances.

Then Bill said: "Can we have a quick word please, guv."

I nodded and closed the cell door enough to prevent anyone from walking straight in.

"We've been wrestling with this for months but we both trust you to do the right thing, so here goes," said Bill.

Bill explained that he and Ben had become 'very close'. But they both had families whom they didn't want to hurt. They were dreading getting out of prison because they knew they'd have to end their relationship or risk humiliation in the underworld... or maybe worse. But neither of them wanted to split up.

Most inmates usually kept these types of friendships secret and returned to their families after their release from prison. Bill was due to get out in 3 months, if he got through the parole board hearing. But Ben wasn't scheduled to be considered for release for another 18 months.

Bill admitted he was seriously considering deliberately blowing his parole application so he could continue living in prison with Ben. They'd both even thought about targeting an inmate inside and murdering him to guarantee they spent the rest of their lives in prison. But they worked out it was a pointless plan because they'd end up in different prisons anyway.

I was relieved by that decision. But despite having dodged the death of an inmate, the whole thing still put me in a terrible predicament because I was duty-bound to report such threats to the prison governor. And even though I knew the governor would do nothing to help them (he wasn't what I would call an empathetic character), I had to inform him. In the end, though, I only mentioned their relationship rather than what I considered to be a meaningless threat. The governor promised me no one would be told about Bill and Ben for the time being, though I knew someone would work everything out sooner or later.

The day after seeing the governor, I noticed some inmates on the wing studying me very closely. Two of them eventually came up to me and asked if the rumours sweeping through the wing that Bill and Ben had fallen in love were true. I refused to be drawn on the subject. It was clear the governor or someone in his office was behind all this. And once a rumour starts inside a prison, it's pretty difficult to stop it spreading like wildfire.

Bill and Ben faced a torrent of vicious, homophobic remarks after that whenever they left their cell. This then made them even more reclusive. Their biggest fear was that their families on the outside might hear about their secret relationship. Some of the other inmates on the wing had known Bill and Ben in the underworld and so their families knew the pair's wives and children.

The next visits by Bill and Ben's families were much harder for the two men to handle. Afterwards, they both confided in me that they feared their wives already knew. Although neither of them had been confronted about it directly, the pressure was clearly getting to them. They seemed anxious and miserable much of the time.

One morning I passed their cell and popped my head in to see how they were. Both were in tears on their bunk beds as Bill read a letter which he told me was from his wife saying she wanted a divorce. He said she hadn't given a reason, so it was impossible to truly know if she was aware of the men's affair. It was only a few weeks before Bill's scheduled release from prison.

Both men told me they'd heard that one particular PO had been telling a lot of people about them on the outside. They asked me if the governor was behind it all. I assured them I didn't think he was, although I was far from convinced.

I sensed the atmosphere change in the cell that morning, so I retreated before they accused me of doing anything against them. That night, I tried to put it all out of my mind over supper with my wife but it was haunting me. I felt that by telling the governor, I was responsible for what was now happening to Bill and Ben.

The following morning, I went out to unlock their door so they could both collect their breakfast packs. I found myself in the wing corridor near their cell, hesitating, as I dreaded how they were going to react to me. For a few moments, I even stopped myself unlocking their cells.

All around me other doors were noisily flying open and inmates were grabbing their breakfast packs before going back in their cells. I finally unlocked Bill and Ben's door without bothering to look through the flap first, which is what you're supposed to do. It felt eerily quiet as I swung open the door.

There was no sign of them anywhere. The cell had been completely cleared out of their belongings. Something had happened overnight, although no one had even bothered to mention a word to me about it. For a split second, I thought maybe they'd committed suicide. But if that had happened, I would have been told when I arrived on the wing that morning.

Then another PO appeared at the doorway. "They got lifted last night on the governor's orders, son," he explained. He told me Bill and Ben had been transferred to separate prisons at opposite ends of the country. I realised that I hadn't been told because the governor thought I might inform them before it happened.

I went to see the governor that morning to complain. He told me to take the day off and think it all through more carefully. I knew there was nothing I could do to change the decision, so I toed the line. I wish I hadn't, but at the same time I'm not sure what I could have done.

Bill and Ben should never have found themselves in such a predicament in the first place. They'd done nothing wrong apart from fall in love. I eventually heard that Bill and his wife ended up back together on his release from prison. Presumably, she never actually found out about her husband's love affair with Ben.

Finding himself facing another year at least before his release from prison, Ben had to reluctantly agree to his wife's demand for the divorce. Not surprisingly, he reached rock bottom shortly after that before eventually starting a relationship with another inmate due for release at the same time as him. But this time he didn't hide his sexuality from anyone and they ended up living together in a city in the West of England.

Sex remains a taboo subject inside most UK prisons, which means these 'crossovers' will keep causing heartache and distress. Yet it could all so easily be avoided if an inmate's sexual choices were not deemed such a sensitive subject.

CHAPTER 10
MUMMY'S BOY

It's always intrigued me why so many mothers of male prison inmates unquestionably support their sons, in spite of the seriousness (and in many cases brutality) of the crimes they've committed. I've come across a number of them down the years. They're usually the first ones in the queue for a pat-down before visiting their beloved boys in prison.

When I was a PO at one of the UK's smaller prisons, I came across one of them who can best be described as the mother of all mothers. She'd stood outside court waving at her boy when he exited a sweat box following his original sentencing. She'd driven across country at high speed to the prison to be there at the gates to greet him when he arrived a few hours later.

One visiting time, this same mother turned up at the prison in a sparkly cocktail dress, black stockings and high heels. She flirted blatantly with one older officer in the visitor reception area. And some of the other POs present that day jokingly said she looked disappointed when one of them told her she wouldn't have to undergo a strip search.

I was on PO duty in the visitor area that day and studied her closely, as she'd become quite a notorious figure by that time. In the visiting hall, dozens of prisoners and their loved ones had just sat down opposite each other on fixed refectory-style tables. Inmates were not supposed to touch their visitors, although we usually allowed them a short hug at the start and finish of a visit. This overdressed mother made a point of giving her son a very lingering kiss on her arrival in the hall.

Some of us already suspected she'd been smuggling drugs and mobile phones into prison during earlier visits. Anyone caught with those types of items risked a custodial sentence, but it was clear this woman didn't care.

Later that day, I was outside her son's cell about to give him a 10-minute warning for lights out when I smelt food. Moments later, I poked my head around the door to find this prisoner and his cellmate each scoffing huge platefuls of homemade spaghetti bolognese. They both grinned at me with guilty expressions on their faces when I advised them lights out time was fast approaching.

This prisoner's cellmate was a classic lifetime criminal type called Sam. He was serving such a long sentence he'd become extremely institutionalised and made it clear to staff that he hoped he never got out. Sam openly broke many prison rules in the hope it would delay his release. This had certain advantages for the wing staff because Sam could be extremely indiscreet about other inmate's activities.

The following morning, I got talking to Sam in the canteen area after he made a point of apologising for acting so 'weirdly' when I'd walked into that cell the previous day. He explained that the spaghetti bolognese they'd been eating had been laced with cannabis and they were stoned. Without any prompting from me, he then said the drugs had been brought into the jail by a prison officer on behalf of his cellmate's mother. I raised my eyebrows in acknowledgement and let Sam continue. He hesitated for a moment before asking me if I'd heard about the mother. I didn't know what he was talking about, so I shook my head.

Sam claimed she was sleeping with one of the wing POs. I asked him if he was joking. He seemed offended and said if I didn't believe him, I should get someone to check out a car park near the prison officer's home that very same night because that was where the pair had sex three times a week in the officer's car. It all sounded like typical jailhouse gossip, just rumours with no substantiation. So I didn't feel I could confront either mother or son. And I certainly wasn't going to go and spy on a car park in my spare time over a bit of gossip. However, I did make a point of studying that inmate and his mother when visiting time came around again the following week.

Within moments of her arrival, I noticed her looking across at the PO whom Sam had claimed she was sleeping with. But again, that wasn't enough evidence to go and tell the governor about my suspicions. So I went back to Sam and asked him for more details about the alleged relationship between the inmate's mother and that PO.

He claimed the mother was supplying drugs and mobile phones to her son often via her same officer lover, who'd taken a lot of items into the jail on her behalf. This time I decided to take Sam seriously and persuaded my wing governor to launch a discreet internal surveillance operation, targeting the son because we felt we'd be unlikely to get enough evidence to confront the mother or her PO lover yet.

We eventually caught him red-handed selling drugs on the wing. After he'd confessed, two senior POs and I gave him a blunt choice. We said we'd put the drug dealing charges to one side if he came clean about his mother and that PO. It was a no-brainer for him because he loathed the PO, even though his mother's sexual relationship with that officer had enabled her son to run his criminal enterprises from inside a prison cell. The son even told us the name of a hotel where the PO and his mother slept together when they were not in his car in a car park.

As part of our agreement with that inmate, his mother was not prosecuted. It was more important to bring a crooked PO to justice than destroy a woman, who actually thought she was just helping her beloved son. At first, the PO flatly denied any relationship with the mother of the inmate. But we then located CCTV footage from the hotel, which clearly showed them arriving and then leaving the premises two hours later.

The officer in question was suspended and eventually fired. I felt he should have been prosecuted for abusing his position in such a blatant manner. But back then, POs like that one were often pushed out of the service as quickly as possible because their behaviour was considered embarrassing. The authorities' priority was to protect the good name of the prison service at all costs. I believe this attitude added to the tension inside prisons, though, because inmates knew that staff didn't have to adhere to the same rules and regulations as them.

CHAPTER 11
THE EXECUTIONER

Contrary to popular opinion, prisons are not filled to the brim with monsters. Most inmates are sad, broken characters who know full well they've made a huge mistake and deserve to pay for it. But occasionally, real psychopaths *do* turn up in prisons and they're often treated with a bizarre combination of hatred and awe.

One such character I came across was a serial killer who'd been convicted of killing more than half a dozen innocent women (although police believed he'd murdered at least 10 more during his 20-year reign of terror). The newspapers had labelled him 'The Executioner' because after raping each victim, he shot them in the head, execution-style, as they knelt pleading for their lives in front of him.

At the time, I'd just started work at a new prison as a regular wing PO. Serial killers hadn't been mentioned much when I was training for this job. Word soon got round at the start of an early shift one morning that this mass murderer was in a holding cell in the reception area. He was waiting to be processed and six of my fellow wing POs were so desperate to escort this serial killer to his cell on the wing that they'd insisted on drawing straws that morning to decide which two would have that 'honour'.

The governor had insisted this inmate was taken straight to his cell and locked in to avoid any confrontations with the general prison population for at least the first 24 hours of his incarceration. But this alleged psychopath certainly wasn't going to strike fear into any of us or the other prisoners. He was about five-foot-five-inches tall, prematurely balding and extremely shy.

As he was escorted to his cell, he kept his head down and didn't seem to notice the dozens of pairs of eyes following his every move. But you could sense a change in the atmosphere on the wing as we walked along the corridor. I'd been in enough prisons by this time to be able to smell trouble brewing. This particular inmate had been given a single cell because it was felt that it would be safer for him. You never know who might want to take the opportunity to dole out punishment on a renowned killer. In any case, most inmates would have refused to share with him.

My first face-to-face encounter with The Executioner occurred the day after he'd arrived as I unlocked his cell at breakfast time. He didn't even look up when I stepped into his cell and told him his food pack was waiting outside for him to pick up. Eventually he nervously stepped outside his cell, grabbed his breakfast pack and darted straight back in.

Later that morning, I was ordered to escort The Executioner down to the yard because the governor had decided it was time he was properly integrated within the general population. Going in the yard was expected to be a big test because it would fully expose him to all the other inmates. They watched us both like hawks as we walked into the yard and strolled around the fenced-off perimeter.

A lot of the wing staff had been convinced some opportunist inmate would have a go at the serial killer just to show what a tough guy he was. There were definitely a few closely examining him out of the corners of their eyes. I had to occasionally guide him with my hand, so we could avoid the most obvious troublemakers in the yard that day. I admit I didn't like even touching him after what he'd been found guilty of doing.

Eventually, The Executioner rolled himself a cigarette, pulled a lighter out and fired it up without looking at any of the other inmates. I stood close by just in case anyone approached. He sucked in huge lungfuls of smoke and began blowing rings out in the direction of the largest group of inmates in the yard. His eyes remained focused on the ground most of the time.

He'd just lit up his second roll-up when I noticed his facial expression hardening up. Then he shut his eyes and began rocking back and forth, still without looking at anyone as he continued smoking. I noticed a small puddle of liquid around his feet. Urine was pouring out of the bottom of his trousers. Some inmates in the yard soon noticed this as well and began pointing it out to their mates. The atmosphere in the yard got much noisier as they began jeering the serial killer.

As the clamour grew, the urine continued steadily streaming out of the bottom of his trousers. I moved closer to The Executioner and ordered him to accompany me back to his cell immediately. He didn't say a word but turned and looked over at the jeering prisoners. He opened his mouth as if he was about to do or say something, but then he closed it again, smiled and looked down.

I sensed something was about to kick off, so I ordered him to hurry up. He opened his mouth a second time and stuck his tongue out at the same inmates watching him from opposite. I grabbed his arm and steered him towards the exit from the yard as some of the inmates began jostling as if they were about to move in our direction.

I ordered him to walk with his head down and warned him not to look at any of them. Surprisingly, we made it to the yard exit in one piece. Once we got to The Executioner's cell, I told him he was going to be locked in immediately for his own safety. He didn't utter a word as I shut the cell door and turned the key. The Executioner did precisely the same thing the following day in the yard, except this time he got even closer to starting a riot before we just managed to exit the yard without being attacked.

I told the governor he was a liability and needed to be properly examined by a mental health expert as he seemed to be deliberately trying to provoke other inmates, and this was very much at odds with the fear he initially showed towards them.

One psychiatrist who eventually saw The Executioner said that he'd wet himself on purpose to upset those other inmates because he wanted to make sure none of them ever tried to be his friend. He also believed that if he offended enough inmates then they might kill him.

Less than 24 hours later, The Executioner was transferred out of my jail and sent to a secure mental facility, where he remained for the rest of his life. If he hadn't been removed from that regular prison environment he would have ended up dead at the hands of some inmate or other, so perhaps it was for the better. I believe he should never have been sent to prison in the first place.

The UK's prisons are littered with these types of characters, even today. Why can't the UK justice system accept that all serial killers must, surely, be insane?

CHAPTER 12
LOFTY

I'd just become a wing PO inside one of the UK's oldest prisons when I came face to face with Lofty for the first time. He was tall and gangly but it wasn't his size that left such an impression on me.

Lofty was a former university lecturer who'd ended up a hopeless alcoholic after being fired from his job 15 years earlier. This guy was so bright, academically speaking, that he could quote lines from Ernest Hemingway and Charles Dickens novels off the top of his head. When I first met him, Lofty seemed very relaxed compared to most other inmates. But he'd been inside at least three times before for relatively minor offences, so he knew the drill only too well.

This time, though, he was serving a sentence for possessing an offensive weapon – a knife. He'd claimed in court that he only carried it as a deterrent. I believed him because he really didn't look capable of hurting another human being. Lofty admitted to me one day on the wing that he preferred being in prison to living outside because it was the only way he could manage to detox. His drug of choice was alcohol, although he never touched the prison hooch, which he said was more akin to poison than alcohol.

When Lofty was a few weeks away from being released this time around, he even tried to smarten himself up by having his long, unkempt hair cut much shorter and shaving off his raggedy beard as well. I and the other POs still noticed that whenever his imminent release was mentioned by either staff or other inmates, he'd go a bit quiet. Lofty was clearly dreading it, even though he never openly admitted this.

Ten days before his release, Lofty went into a complete meltdown after attending an illicit hooch party in a neighbouring cell, where he got completely hammered. I actually found him swaying in a corridor and helped guide him to his cell so he could sleep it off. There had been absolutely no point in disciplining Lofty, despite the irritation shown by two other nearby POs who seemed unable to appreciate that punishing Lofty was playing right into his hands anyway, because he was looking for any excuse not to leave prison.

The hangover Lofty suffered the following day no doubt added to the condition of his mental health. Lofty was shuffling around the main rec area mumbling to himself about where he was going to get his next drink. When I tried to help by offering to call in a prison counsellor for him to speak to, Lofty's face darkened and he said he'd kill me and the counsellor if I ever did that. One of those same older POs from the previous day overheard the threat and told me I had to report it to the wing governor. But I insisted Lofty was only joking and ignored him.

But after that other officer had left, Lofty insisted he was being serious and that he couldn't be held responsible for what he might do to another inmate or member of staff, as he was struggling so much about being released from prison. I managed to get him to calm down and persuaded him to agree to a transfer to the seg wing, away from the general prison population. This meant he'd be held in a single cell, which would give him a chance to properly sober up and maybe even mentally prepare himself for his release back into the real world.

Within a couple of days, Lofty insisted his mental health problems had eased off and he thanked me profusely for putting him in the seg unit. I was well aware he could switch moods in a nanosecond, so I decided to still keep an eye on him. I remember locking Lofty's cell door that evening and glancing through the glass slit in the door to make sure he was okay. He looked up at me with an empty expression and a forced smile but little else.

* * *

I was getting dressed at home the following morning before going in for work when the governor's deputy called. He said Lofty was refusing to come out of his cell unless I talked to him. He wouldn't speak to anyone else. The governor's deputy said they didn't have enough staff on duty to go into his cell and force him out, so I needed to get in as quickly as possible.

I wasn't surprised. When I'd left Lofty the previous night, I knew he was going downhill fast. An hour later I got to the prison and made my way straight to Lofty's cell in the seg wing. It had remained locked since I'd gone home the previous evening. Lofty's only communication had been through the cell door with a duty wing officer earlier that morning.

As I approached the cell, I noticed the small glass pane in the door had been smeared with something on the inside, and it was impossible to see into the cell. Then I realised it must be excrement. I knocked very gently on the door after deciding it was better for the moment to talk to him from the corridor, rather than unlock the door and walk in. Lofty answered immediately and I realised he was standing just on the other side of the door slit.

He apologised profusely about what had happened, but said he felt he had no choice because he didn't want to be released from prison. He told me he was terrified that once he was back outside, he'd immediately go back on the booze, and he really didn't want that.

Lofty was so immersed in his own world that no matter what I said, he didn't seem to hear me. He just continued mumbling relentlessly about his problems. I have noticed during my many years in the service that mentally challenged inmates often do this. Their world becomes the only world that matters to them and they really cannot see the wood for the trees.

I listened patiently as Lofty listed all the reasons why he didn't want to leave prison, even though I'd heard them all before. Eventually, he ran out of things to say and stopped talking. The smell of excrement by this time was almost overpowering, even though the cell door remained locked. I let the silence hang in the air over us for a few moments, so that the enormity of what he'd done might properly sink in.

"I'm so sorry about this," he whispered, from the other side of the door.

I asked him to wait and promised I'd be back soon. Less than five minutes later, I returned in a white prison-issue chem-suit with two colleagues similarly attired. We looked more like comic book astronauts than prison officers.

Lofty sounded very receptive as I spoke to him through the cell door again and explained that we were coming in to clear everything up. Before unlocking the door and entering, I ordered Lofty to face the wall at the other end of his cell and not move. I was only certain he had obeyed when I heard his voice and knew he was further away than earlier.

I held my breath as much as I could and walked in. Rotting brown faeces were smeared all over the walls and Lofty stood completely naked with his back towards us covered from head to foot in his own excrement. Despite the almost overwhelming smell, I managed to handcuff Lofty and, with the help of three colleagues, we removed him from the cell without any resistance. Smears of Lofty's excrement covered our white suits as we guided Lofty – who was bent forward – along a corridor towards the holding cell next to the main entrance of the seg wing.

As we moved along that corridor, Lofty asked me what punishment he could expect to receive for his dirty protest.

"None," I said, firmly.

He looked mortified.

"But..." he responded.

"Lofty, mate," I said. "You can't avoid being released by doing this. You need to face up to dealing with the outside world. I'm sorry but that's the way it is."

Lofty nodded and shrugged his shoulders. Perhaps not so surprisingly, Lofty didn't last long in the outside world. He got in a drunken pub brawl and ended up in a much cushier open prison serving a one-year sentence.

This time he didn't bother with a dirty protest as his release day approached. Instead, he chose a more effective way to avoid the real world by hanging himself in his cell. I was really sad to hear that. Today, Lofty would hopefully have got proper counselling inside and outside prison for his alcohol addiction and maybe his life wouldn't have been so cruelly wasted.

CHAPTER 13
ODD MAN OUT

Rookie prison officer JT, aged just 23, shuffled nervously into the prison I was serving in (my fifth so far) for his first day and most of us knew almost immediately he was not cut out for the job. I remember his eyes snapping nervously around the wing as I accompanied him on a first day tour with another colleague. I kept telling JT to keep his eyes to himself at all times but he couldn't stop looking twitchily at all the inmates. When I told him to start locking inmates' cells for a lockdown, I noticed his hands shaking.

But it wasn't just the inmates who unnerved JT. He soon began pissing off a lot of other POs, too. Many of the older ones weren't exactly empathetic at the best of times. They labelled JT as a 'shit-scared kid' and the majority of them went out of their way *not* to help him.

As a result, JT quickly found himself on his own a lot of the time, which wasn't good for someone as vulnerable and inexperienced as he was. And, of course, after weeks of clearly being out of his depth, the inmates started taking even more interest in JT. Prisoners would encircle him in the canteen and out in the yard. One of the golden rules of this game is to never allow inmates to think they're intimidating or controlling you in any way. They'd pretend to be laughing and joking when they were really testing him out.

The first couple of times it happened, I wandered into the crowd and broke it up without reprimanding JT in front of the inmates. Afterwards I told him he needed to step away the moment they approached, otherwise they'd start thinking they 'owned' him.

After I'd had to rescue JT a third time, my senior wing officer pulled me aside in the locker room and ordered me to stop helping JT. It was a difficult moment for me because I didn't want to throw JT to the wolves. But I also didn't want to end up as isolated as he so clearly was.

After that, watching JT on the wing was like waiting for a car crash to happen. One time I was strolling through the staff car park after a shift when one of the old-school POs who'd long since stopped talking to JT walked up to me.

"A fiver says JT will end up being shanked by one of our resident psychos," he said.

I brushed off the comment without saying much. But, after a night of thinking about it, the following morning I pulled JT aside in the locker room and suggested that maybe he wasn't cut out for the job. He looked crestfallen when I said it and walked away without even answering me. He refused to talk to me again after that.

A couple of weeks later, JT was stabbed with a biro in the eye by one young inmate who claimed that JT had been spreading rumours around the prison that he was a paedophile. It was a deliberate set-up. Someone had wound that inmate up, so he'd have a go at JT. JT's eye was saved and many staff members hoped that surviving the attack might give him more respect inside prison.

But instead JT suffered some form of PTSD and he turned into an even more terrified version of himself before the stabbing. One time, I heard him weeping in a stall in the staff toilet, although I didn't say anything to the rest of the team because I didn't want to humiliate him. Inmates began sniggering behind his back again and many officers continued coldly ignoring him.

I eventually managed to get JT to start talking to me again and persuaded him to meet me for a pint in a local pub after work. I advised him to leave the service before something even more serious happened to him. But like before, JT got upset by my criticism and stormed out of the pub. Unfortunately, that would be one of the last times we had a proper conversation. I knew that JT still lived at home with his widowed mother and there was a lot of financial pressure on him to support them both. Maybe that was why he was so afraid of quitting?

Out on the wing, perceptive prisoners were picking up on his fragile emotional state and putting him under even more pressure by insulting him both to his face and behind his back. On one occasion, I saw an inmate trip JT up as he walked down the metal stairs in the middle of the wing. Luckily, he only fell a couple of steps, brushed himself down and carried on as if nothing had happened. JT didn't even have the courage to reprimand the inmate after what happened. A classic golden rule of being a PO is never let prisoners get away with anything like that.

I heard from a secretary in the administration office that JT's mother was seriously ill at home with cancer, so, although I couldn't ask him, I began to suspect that was why he seemed so distracted a lot of the time. Then, a few days later, an inmate accused JT of making advances towards him. The accusation was patently false but some inmates and POs began gossiping that JT had forced himself on the inmate.

I knew JT better than any of them. He was too scared all the time to ever embark on an affair with an inmate. In any case, I didn't think he was gay (though admittedly I hadn't asked him as it wasn't relevant to me). I could have ignored him and said it wasn't my problem, but I felt I had to do something, so I spoke to the governor off the record in the hope none of my colleagues would find out. I told the governor that JT had a lot of problems and he was in a highly vulnerable state, and should somehow be assessed for this, for his own wellbeing. The governor said he couldn't do anything because JT had refused to agree to a medical examination and the PO union was backing him up.

A few days after my conversation with the governor, JT didn't show up for work. It was the first time he'd ever gone missing from the job. No one apart from me seemed to give a shit. At the end of my shift that day, I went by JT's home to see if he was okay, but no one answered the front door when I rang the bell at his house.

After a few minutes, I peered through a front window to see if there was any sign of anyone. There was a bottle of pills lying on the floor upturned with tablets scattered all over the carpet. I called the police and half an hour later we got into the house and discovered his elderly mother dead in an upstairs bedroom. She'd finally succumbed to cancer and JT seemed to have fled the house after discovering her.

He was never seen or heard of again. Most people think he left the country. I think it's much more likely he committed suicide. Whatever the real outcome, the prison service shouldn't have recruited JT in the first place because he was so clearly not cut out for the job.

There was and still is an overriding mentality within the service that people will always eventually learn the ropes and end up being good at their job, even when the opposite is plainly obvious for all to see. Unless prisons overhaul their training and recruitment policies, problem officers like JT will be swept under the carpet or, worse still, they'll end up in big trouble while on the job. Mental health problems inside prisons have been ignored for centuries. Today, it's an acceptable topic for discussion, but that doesn't mean the service is able to cope with it.

CHAPTER 14
TREATMENT

Some of my more old-fashioned colleagues when I was a PO were even convinced that ill mental health was nothing more than an excuse for inmates to break the rules. It's an easy way to avoid responsibility for the entire subject, although I acknowledge that one of the biggest dilemmas for any PO on a wing is whether an inmate is pretending to be mentally ill. Prisoners sometimes make out they're 'going crazy' to force a transfer or avoid work.

And I'd quickly discovered that, as a PO, I was often expected to make decisions based on gut instinct rather than call in the experts with medical knowledge and training. That in itself seemed dangerous because if I got it wrong, I could be putting other inmates and staff in danger if that inmate had some type of breakdown.

I learned all this the hard way shortly after arriving at a new prison, when I was still a wing PO. The inmate in question was a notoriously dangerous prisoner whose hair-trigger temper had landed him in the prison seg unit for the best part of five years. This particular inmate had been allowed back into the general prison population just before I started work on the wing. But none of the staff seemed interested in what had caused all his anger. He was just seen as 'a pain in the arse', as one PO put it.

My first encounter with him came during a mid-morning recreation break when I was one of six POs on duty in the yard. He was smoking a rollie in a corner, well away from all the other prisoners. Although I'd been warned about him, he seemed calm and self-controlled, despite numerous other inmates looking right at him. When three prisoners brushed past him provocatively a few minutes later, he simply moved out of their way without comment. I was so intrigued by this that I decided to keep a close eye on him.

The following lunchtime, I noticed him sitting at a table on his own in the canteen, mumbling to himself. It seemed to me that other inmates were deliberately avoiding sitting near him. I wondered at first if he was feigning madness to get a transfer. But he was talking so quietly to himself, with no one else around to hear, that it just didn't seem like he could be faking it. But then when I approached him at the table, he looked up and immediately stopped talking to himself. Maybe that meant he was pretending to be mad after all?

When I asked him if he was okay, he nodded at me reluctantly and said that he was fine. But when I moved away from the table, he began mumbling to himself again, this time much louder than before. From what I heard, he seemed to be discussing his own inner thoughts with himself. I recognised that a lot of what he was saying was about me and the other staff members. He kept saying he hated us all and how he wanted to kill us. After realising this, I began to wonder if what was in his mind amounted in any way to a credible threat to our safety.

Later that day, I informed my wing governor that I thought this inmate should be seen by a mental health expert to find out what was wrong with him. The senior officer immediately said he thought the inmate was probably faking it, like so many of them did. It was hard to counter his argument because I had nothing more than a hunch to go on, and it's difficult to convince others of the validity of what you think is going on inside someone else's mind. Still, I didn't feel I could just stand by and watch a man disintegrate in front of my very eyes. And to me there was also a real danger he might turn those muttering threats into an attack on the staff and other inmates.

I couldn't go over the head of my wing governor without it being perceived as an act of betrayal, so I started doing my own research into what this inmate's behaviour might really mean. To me, he seemed close to the edge of insanity. After taking notes and then relaying it to a therapist friend of mine, he warned me that the inmate was showing all the symptoms of someone having an ongoing 'psychotic episode'.

The therapist predicted that this condition would escalate if measures were not taken to deal with it through prescription drugs and intense psychological counselling. But despite this, the prison administration still refused to even acknowledge this inmate had ill mental health.

About two weeks after initially reporting my fears to my wing governor, the inmate was severely beaten up by three prisoners whom he'd insulted while he was speaking aloud to himself in the canteen. Despite ending up in the prison infirmary with a broken arm and six fractured ribs, the inmate refused to give evidence against the men responsible. He even said he deserved to be beaten up because he knew he'd upset them by constantly talking to himself especially at night, when he was keeping many inmates near his cell awake with his muttering.

Not long after he got out of the infirmary, I found the inmate talking to himself in an otherwise empty shower room. It turned out that all the other inmates had refused to go in there with him because he was behaving so strangely. Yet, even after all this, my wing governor still refused to do anything to help him. He remained convinced the inmate was faking an 'episode'. I suspected that this senior officer just couldn't be bothered to fill in the paperwork in order to get this inmate proper mental health supervision.

I knew that it would only be a matter of time before this inmate was involved in something even more serious than the earlier beating, and then, one lunchtime a few days later, I walked into the canteen to find him surrounded by six other prisoners who were accusing him of insulting them. I explained to them that he was sick and needed medical attention and eventually managed to get them to step back. I then escorted the inmate back to his cell. After locking him in, I had one last look at him through the flap in the door. I remember, he glanced over at me and winked. That completely threw me.

After all these weeks of believing he was in trouble, I began to doubt if he was sick after all. That evening, I told the night duty POs not to bother him and that I'd deal with him when I was back on the wing the following morning.

Less than 12 hours later I arrived back at his cell and unlocked it so he could retrieve his breakfast pack from his doorstep. When he didn't appear, I pushed the door further open to find him with his head under the water in the lavatory bowl. I leaned down and pulled him out, grabbed him under both his arms and dragged his limp body on to the bed. He'd tried to drown himself, but hadn't succeeded.

I slapped his face a few times and he suddenly came to. He looked broken as he thanked me and then pleaded for me to get him help. This time, I insisted he was committed to a mental health unit. After what had happened, none of my fellow officers objected.

There was an important issue at play here, too. If that inmate hadn't almost killed himself, then the prison service would never have even woken up to his serious mental health issues.

These instances needed to be tackled more proactively. And the only way I could make a difference was to try and climb the service's promotion ladder sooner rather than later.

CHAPTER 15
DRIFTING APART

After a while, the prison service gets so ingrained in your soul that you end up living, eating and breathing it, to the detriment of the rest of your life. I often found myself struggling to switch off from what I'd seen and done during a shift. A lot of POs I've known down the years have always insisted they never talked about their work at home. But I always believed repressing your feelings in such ways was not very healthy.

I used to share a few things with my family as I wanted them to appreciate the reality of what I did for a living and ensure my job didn't become like the ultimate elephant in the room. I held back on the nastier stuff, though, because I didn't want my family constantly worrying that something might happen to me at work. Ultimately, though, the real problem is that the work–life balance of most prison officers is ludicrously one-sided. For many, a shift with overtime inside a prison can often amount to more hours than they actually spend at home over a 24-hour period.

The wife of a PO once told me: "My old man gets home grumpy because of all the bad shit he's just been through at work. He never wants to talk to me about it, so how can I be sympathetic to what he's going through? We have to tread on eggshells so as not to upset him.

"Next morning, he goes to work still grumpy because he's dreading another day of abuse and the threat of violence. It's a never-ending vicious circle."

In reality, there is absolutely nothing that can prepare your family for what to expect when you work in the prison service. If I had my time again, I'd have warned my loved ones that there would be moments when I wouldn't be able to cope with some everyday domestic stuff because of what I'd been through at work.

My own wife hadn't been keen on me staying in the prison service after we met. After we'd just got married, she told me I wasn't tough enough to cope with it. That comment made me even more determined to do it. I did, however, avoid telling my wife and family some of the classic statistics associated with my new career, including a life expectancy level that was 15 years below the country's average and a 40 per cent higher suicide rate than any other public service occupation. POs also have a higher rate of heart attacks and alcoholism, as well as a propensity for ill mental health, with conditions including PTSD, anxiety and depression.

When my wife and I had many of our discussions about why I was continuing as a prison officer, I usually told her that it was my calling in life. And when I did that, she (admittedly with some reluctance) stepped back and continued to let me get on with it, which I will always be grateful to her for doing.

Often during the first few years I was a PO, I'd find myself working 60-hour weeks because most prisons at that time were so under-staffed. Unfortunately, night shifts automatically put my wife and me on opposite daily schedules. We even frequently ended up having different days off from our jobs and then child-care issues kicked in and it got even harder. More often than not, we ended up like strangers passing in the night.

After that, I guess inevitably, my wife accused me of being married to my job rather than her. She had a good point. I'd thrown myself into my career and maybe I'd lost sight of the other sides of my life in my determination to make a contin-ued success of my chosen career.

One evening I shed a few tears explaining to my wife how I'd managed to talk an inmate out of jumping off the roof of the prison gym building that morning. It's only now that I realise just telling her this was manipulative of me, and that I was trying to involve her in my job and its hardships in order to help her better understand my position.

She would react to things like this by also asking me pointedly why I'd joined the prison service when it wasn't exactly well paid. We'd just had two children, so money was tight all the time and I could see where she was coming from, not that the comments helped much. When she asked me how I could deal with all the violence inside prison, I just shrugged my shoulders because I felt awkward discussing it.

My marriage felt more and more like it was battling for survival. I didn't want my job to destroy it but I also wasn't prepared to walk away from my career, especially after I'd invested so much in it both practically and emotionally. I think all my wife really wanted was for me to be safe at home with her and the kids, and what she heard about my job suggested it really wasn't safe.

I remember one morning, I was already up and ironing my uniform in the front room when I noticed my wife watching me with a worried expression on her face. When I asked her what was wrong she said, 'Nothing.' I knew she was lying.

Later, as I strolled down the garden path towards my motorbike parked on the street, I remember looking back at the front window. For the first time ever, my wife wasn't there waving me goodbye.

When I got home that evening, she made a point of saying how much I'd changed since we'd first fallen in love and married. She then repeated what she'd first told me at the beginning of my career; that I was 'too nice' to be in the prison service.

It was hard being on the front line in the prison service and then coming home to such criticism. If this had happened today, maybe I would have sought out the help of an established support network for prison officers' families but they didn't exist back then.

Throughout this period, I remained determined not to let my problems at home affect my work. Being inside a prison each morning began to feel like a relief compared to the atmosphere at home.

At a party once, one of my wife's friends asked me some very inquisitive questions about the prison where I worked.

I pointed out that I was unable to speak about those things because of the confidentiality agreement I'd signed at the start of my career.

Afterwards my wife accused me of disrespecting her friends. I told her I didn't really care what they thought. To make things worse, later that evening – after all my wife's guests had departed and we'd gone to bed – someone knocked on our front door.

I got out of bed and grabbed a small canister of pepper spray which I always kept in a bedside table drawer. I remember noticing my wife watching me as I put it in my pocket and crept down the stairs. The caller turned out to be a dinner guest who'd forgotten their mobile phone. That incident hung in the air like a bad smell for days.

We eventually had a terrible row and she told me she didn't want to be married to a man who carried pepper spray around in his pocket. That's when I knew she was looking for an excuse to end our marriage. But I didn't say anything other than to apologise for having the pepper spray in the bedside table.

So I plodded on, hopeful that eventually our difficulties would sort themselves out and we'd still end up living happily ever after. I even requested a transfer to a prison closer to my home in the hope it might help improve our relationship, as that would enable me to spend more time with my family.

The only position available was as a PO in a women's jail, which was a 20-minute drive from our house. But even that caused problems. My wife didn't like the idea of me working in a women's prison and was annoyed I hadn't consulted her before accepting the job. Despite this, I was determined to make the best of it. I soon discovered that female prisoners could often be much more challenging than men. The threat of violence may have been virtually non-existent but the pain and anguish suffered by so many women inmates was omnipresent.

Most had separation issues when it came to their families on the outside. Clearly many of them couldn't 'tough it out' like a lot of men and found that prison even impacted seriously on their maternal instincts. They did seem to trust POs much more, though, and this contributed to a much better all-round relationship between staff and inmates.

My wife soon began commenting on how much more relaxed I'd become after starting at the women's prison, and seemed happy about this, but she also continually asked me how attractive the inmates and female staff members were. I tried to assure her there was nothing to worry about. She didn't look as if she believed me whenever I said that. I even talked to my wife about some of the actual inmates to try and put her mind at rest. That didn't seem to help, either.

At the women's prison, one of the female officers who worked alongside me on our wing noticed I seemed a bit down one morning. I ended up confiding in her that I was having a few problems at home and some of it seemed to be down to working in a women's prison.

She said she'd been through similar problems with her husband when she'd worked at a men's prison. She'd tried to reassure him but they constantly rowed about it and in the end they got divorced. This set off even more alarm bells in my head.

Back home, my wife was out alone socialising more and more while I'd insisted on babysitting our two children. I was determined not to miss out on their upbringing, although it was an uphill struggle because I found it hard adjusting to the 'normal' side of my life after spending the day inside a prison filled with criminals.

But those domestic issues did help me to further appreciate the plight of many of the female inmates inside that prison where I was serving at that time. In the end, I coped at home by splitting myself into two people in a sense. One was a caring, patient PO inside a women's prison while the other was a somewhat timid husband, scared that any wrong move might lead to the disintegration of my family unit.

CHAPTER 16
ESCAPE MODE

At that women's prison, a lot of inmates generally found it especially hard to come to terms with the crimes they'd committed. I encountered one woman who'd murdered her two teenage daughters. Despite being in prison, she was in complete denial about what she'd done and continually tried to convince other inmates she was innocent.

Every month, a special 'family day' was held to allow inmates to see their children and spouses to help maintain those relationships. These 'family days' were often highly emotional events for imprisoned mothers. In the week before family day, a sword of Damocles hung over prisoners because if they misbehaved in any way they wouldn't be allowed to attend family day.

The inmate who killed her daughters had pushed for her one surviving son to come into the prison on family day. I was astounded. She'd cold-bloodedly murdered his two sisters because – it had been alleged in court – she was jealous of their good looks. I had no right to interfere with the prison authorities' decision to permit her son to attend family day. But at the same time, I couldn't understand why he'd even agreed to visit his mother after what she'd done to his sisters. It was clear to me she must have been controlling him, even after the appalling crimes that she'd committed.

When I asked my female guard friend at the prison if I should make my feelings known to the governor, she pointed out that maybe this was part of both mother and son's rehabilitation process. It was a fair point. Maybe I was the one being controlling here.

Later that same afternoon, though, I overheard the same woman inmate on the phone in the prison corridor talking to her son. It sounded like she was getting him to smuggle something in for her. I stopped just around the corner from the public phones and listened more closely to exactly what was being said, without her knowing.

I heard her voice harden as she reprimanded him about something. Then she said that unless he came to see her, she'd tell the police about his own involvement in the murders. That convinced me my suspicions had been right all along and I needed to go and tell the governor what I'd heard.

The son's visitor permit for family day was immediately cancelled after I told the governor what I suspected. I heard from another wing officer that the mother went into a complete meltdown after she was told.

Two days later, she tried to kill herself. I was convinced it was down to me and was feeling terrible, even though the doctor told me it was just a half-hearted attempt, so was probably more of a cry for help than anything else.

A week after this, I walked into her cell after other inmates had complained that her loud wailing at night had been keeping other inmates awake. She didn't even look up when I entered and said nothing after I mentioned the complaints and asked her to stop.

As I turned to leave the cell, she muttered: "I know you stopped my boy visiting."

I didn't respond and continued walking out of the cell before calmly locking the door. I leaned down to check on her through the flap. When I opened it, she was pressed up so close to it that I could see the bloodshot whites of her eyes.

She then mouthed the words: "I know it was you." I shut the flap with a bang and walked off up the corridor.

For the following couple of weeks, I managed to avoid any direct contact with the inmate and thought it would be forgotten soon enough. At home, my marriage problems were worsening. But like so many couples, we were both trying to avoid being the first one to instigate a move to end the relationship.

Back at the prison, I was in the staff locker room for the early shift when the reception officer informed me the new governor wanted to see me. As I entered his office, he was clasping some paper with a grim expression and ordered me to sit down. He explained that the prison had intercepted some letters written by the woman who killed her daughters to her best friend. They detailed an affair she claimed to be having inside prison with me. I was lost for words.

The governor tried to reassure me he thought she was lying. But I could tell from the hesitant tone of his voice, that he wasn't entirely convinced. I immediately told him she was getting revenge because she'd found out that I had stopped her son from visiting. The governor said he was duty-bound to investigate the allegations but assured me he would not be talking to the inmate at this stage.

Despite the governor's doubt, I had to be suspended from work until those investigations were completed. Naively, I hadn't seen that one coming. I should have known how the system worked. I'd have to bite my lip and wait for the process to be completed.

I was back home before lunchtime that day after my suspension, so I sat down with my wife and told her about the allegations by the inmate and all the background to try and explain why that prisoner might be out to get revenge.

Initially, my wife seemed sympathetic but then she asked me if the inmate was attractive. I refused to answer because it was such a stupid question. When I suggested lunch in a local pub to further discuss everything, she turned it down and announced she'd already arranged to meet a friend, so I couldn't even really solve the issue. I was so desperate to talk to someone that I called my friend, the female guard, who was on a day off with her children. She was very understanding and assured me that I'd soon be in the clear and back at work.

That afternoon my wife returned from her lunch in an even uglier mood. She said she could no longer cope with the constant threats connected to my job at the prison and she didn't want to spend her life with me anymore.

I realised that my suspension from prison had been the perfect opportunity for her to do what she'd been planning for months and leave me. I persuaded her to stop and think about everything she was saying for half an hour while I had a shower and tried to sort my head out. After that, we could continue the conversation.

Exactly half an hour later, I walked back into the sitting room to find her crying. I tried to console her but she brushed me off and confessed that she'd fallen in love with someone else.

My world completely fell apart that afternoon. I'd just been suspended from work and now my wife had announced she was having an affair. It couldn't get much worse than that. She left the house immediately that afternoon with our kids to see her lover, leaving me alone in our house. I barely slept a wink that night and spent the entire following day in bed staring at the ceiling, wondering how it had all come to this.

Early the following morning the phone rang. It was the governor. My heart sank as I presumed it was more bad news.

"We've dropped the investigation," he said. "She's admitted she made it all up."

I couldn't believe it had happened so quickly. I'd thought it would take weeks. When I asked the governor what happened, he explained that my female guard friend had persuaded the inmate to admit she'd made it all up because she'd been so upset that her son's visitor permission for that family day had been withdrawn.

This actually marked the beginning of a new life for me. I was convinced fate had played a hand because now I saw the way clear to push for promotion, having finally turned the corner when it came to my domestic life.

For those that want to know, my wife ended up much happier with someone who wasn't connected to the prison service. I eventually fell in love with someone who was in the service and understood (and accepted) every aspect of the job. But more on that later. And, at the end of the day, I have that murderous inmate to thank for it all.

CHAPTER 17
TWISTED JUSTICE

My final job as a wing officer at a men's prison was filled with many mixed emotions. My application for promotion had been processed remarkably quickly after I attended a prison service interview which went well, even though I'd openly expressed my opinions about improving the system.

However, I was determined to continue to perform my PO duties to the best of my abilities until I left that final post. I'd become quite protective towards one inmate who'd suffered racism and physical threats on a regular basis, ever since he'd arrived at this prison a couple of months earlier.

He'd originally been sentenced for his alleged role in the murder of a rival gang member on a council estate. He always insisted he'd done nothing apart from being present during the attack. He even claimed he'd tried to stop it. He'd then been arrested alongside other gang members who committed the actual murder when police raided a house where they were hiding out following the killing. When he first arrived in prison, his claims were considered fanciful and that he was just another inmate insisting he was innocent when he was not.

However, I started taking his claims more seriously when two members from the same gang, who were also in the prison, began threatening to kill him. They seemed obsessed that he might speak out against them.

The inmate eventually became too scared to leave his cell. On the few occasions he went in the exercise yard, he was shunned by many other prisoners. It was the same at mealtimes in the canteen. He just sat on his own in a corner most days. Clearly, word had got around that he might rat on the gang.

When the threats against him increased, prison administrators decided he was safer in a single cell. He refused this offer, though, because he believed that the other gang members would presume he'd informed on them in exchange for a better cell. If this happened, he thought they'd go after his family on the council estate where they all lived.

I spent many hours over a period of two or three months trying to convince this inmate he should give evidence against the other gang members. He steadfastly rejected my suggestion, despite still insisting he was innocent of any involvement in the murder.

One time, we were talking on the wing corridor when he told me there were some mobile phone photos which showed three of the gang members killing another victim three weeks before the murder they'd all been convicted of. This inmate could be clearly seen in the background of one of the photos. He told me that another member of the gang had taken the pictures because they wanted him to be implicated in the murder, so that he didn't ever give evidence against them. No wonder he was so scared of them.

Back on the wing – which he continued to refuse to be transferred from – the earlier threats turned into actual beatings. While I tried to get the names of the perpetrators out of him, he wouldn't name his attackers in case his family were punished.

All of this put me in a very difficult position. I'd been told certain things by this inmate that I really should have reported, but I couldn't tell anyone because it might lead to either the inmate or his family being seriously hurt or even killed.

In the middle of this, my first promotion was officially confirmed and I was ordered to begin my management training at a much bigger and more challenging prison almost immediately. My elation about the new job was tinged with concern for that vulnerable inmate. Would he survive without me watching his back for him? When I told him I was leaving, he bravely wished me well.

In a perfect world, I would have passed on my concerns to another PO, so they kept an eye on this inmate. But it's not really as simple as that when it comes to the staff and inmates. I was worried that whoever I told would go straight to the governor, irrespective of the inmate's wishes, and the gang would be sure to hear about it and go after his family.

A couple of days before my actual departure from that prison, I found the inmate shaking in a corner of his cell afraid to come out for recreation. He'd been informed in a phone call that a death threat had been made to his family on the outside.

He was convinced that once I left prison, they'd kill him or a family member. In the end, I managed to persuade the two officers in charge of his corridor to let him stay in his cell during rec that day, though I didn't tell them the full story of what was happening. Then I went straight to the governor and asked if this inmate could be transferred to another jail. I told the governor that I feared for his safety once I'd left that prison.

Unsurprisingly, the governor wasn't very sympathetic. He said that because the inmate was in prison for murder, there could be no preferential treatment for him. But by this time, the gang members were directly threatening death on him and his family if he ever mentioned his predicament to anyone.

On the drive to work on my last day at that prison, I couldn't stop thinking about all this. As I got changed for my final wing-duty shift, another PO congratulated me on my impending move and asked me why I looked so miserable about it, and I couldn't really explain.

About 10 minutes into my shift, I came face to face with that inmate in the corridor just after the prisoners had been allowed to step out of their cells to collect their breakfast packs. He looked at me and nodded but we didn't say anything else and he just grabbed the food pack and darted back into his cell before I locked the door again.

After doing that, I stopped and opened the flap and looked in. He glanced across at me and nodded again but still said nothing else. Just seeing him there in the cell that morning sent a shiver up my spine. It felt to me as if I was sending him to his own death.

An hour later, all the cells were unlocked for rec in the exercise yard. The majority of inmates surged down the corridor moments later in the rush for some fresh air. But the inmate I'd tried to help wouldn't leave his cell, so I entered it to speak to him.

"I bet you can't wait to get out of this shithole," he said to me as I stood by the entrance to the cell. I was about to say something when a senior wing PO passed in the corridor by the cell. This particular guard was very old school and had already reprimanded me for spending too much time trying to help the more needy inmates.

I moved away from the entrance to the cell, but the PO stopped and asked why the inmate wasn't going to the yard. I explained that he didn't want to. He immediately walked into the cell and ordered the inmate to go to the yard.

"You need some fuckin' exercise, son," he barked.

The inmate brushed past me as he shuffled dejectedly off down the corridor towards the stairs that led to the yard. I stood at an upstairs window in the corridor watching him enter the yard. At first no one looked at him. It was as if he were invisible. I noticed a group of men, including two of the gang members who took part in the murder that got him jailed, start watching him.

He headed in the opposite direction from them towards the other end of the yard but two men from the same group cut off his exit route. This forced him to stop by a chain-link fence. His hands shook as he tried to light a cigarette. The gang members watched him closely but held back because they knew the cameras were following their every move.

I continued watching from my lookout post, partly in the hope that my attention would prevent anything from happening. I was relieved when the bell for the end of rec time went off and that inmate was left still standing, untouched. Then, as the prisoners began heading for the exit, I noticed three men surround him. They said something to him and he tried to move away from them.

As he tried to flee, one of them tripped him up and he fell on to the concrete. All of a sudden, five more men crowded around him as he lay on the ground, so I couldn't see what was happening. Two guards who were close by in the yard immediately headed towards them, and they began dispersing.

It was only then I noticed him crumpled up on the ground. He didn't seem to be moving. I used my walkie-talkie to alert the staff inside the yard that something had happened and headed down there. I arrived in the yard to find two officers trying to move him while checking for vital signs of life. There were smears of blood on the concrete. It was clear he'd been shanked.

Half an hour later, I visited the infirmary to find out how he was. Although the wounds turned out to be superficial, it was clear the other gang members had given that inmate a message that they were watching him and would kill him if they wanted to.

My heart sank when the nurse in the infirmary told me that he'd be fine and would be released back on to the wing before lunchtime. I'd hoped he'd be kept in there at least overnight, so that it gave me a chance to try and talk the governor into transferring him.

I saw him again when I was on canteen duty that lunchtime. He had a black eye, a plaster over his eyebrow and a bandage over his arm where they'd shanked him. He was sitting on his own in a corner of the refectory.

He looked up at me and I was about to look back at him when I noticed two of the gang members watching me and sneering. There were just five hours left of my final shift in that prison. I could have tried to make sure I didn't bump into that inmate again that day, at least to avoid the guilt I was feeling. But that would have been cowardly. I wanted to help him until the very last minute I left the prison at the end of that day.

I owed him my protection at the very least. So about an hour after lunch, I walked up the corridor to where his cell was and glanced in through the open door to see if he was okay. All I could see were his feet on the bed. I paused for a moment, hesitant about entering the cell.

His feet didn't seem to be moving, so I stepped into the cell with a sense of trepidation. He was curled up on the bed, not moving but definitely breathing. He didn't even look up at first as I moved closer, then, as I was about to lean down, he finally turned around and said: "Help me, please." I couldn't offer anything, and so said nothing. This realisation was so unnerving that I remember my hands shaking as I locked his cell door after seeing him.

Within a week of my departure from that prison, he'd been beaten up three times by other inmates. The governor was left with no choice but to transfer him to another prison.

Three years later, that same inmate won an appeal and had his conviction overturned. The gang members were also prosecuted for the other murder after photos of it ended up in the hands of the police.

But giving evidence against the other gang members came at a very high price for the inmate and his family. They were put in a witness protection programme and had to move to another part of the UK.

Some years later, I received a letter from him thanking me for trying so hard to help. But reading between the lines, I suspected that he probably wished he'd just served his sentence in the end because then he and his family wouldn't have had to uproot to somewhere that turned their lives upside down.

I was deeply impacted by what happened to that inmate. Had I allowed my ambition to influence the way I handled him? I needed to tread very carefully in future if I was going to climb that promotion ladder.

PART TWO

THE GOVERNOR

*"The best way to keep a prisoner from escaping is
to make sure he never knows he's in prison."*

FYODOR DOSTOEVSKY

CHAPTER 18
THE EXPERIMENT

I knew when I chose to try and climb the prison service ladder that I'd be put through some difficult tests before I got anywhere near being an actual governor. Prison service management training is supposed to expose you to unique situations that require thinking on your feet. That can mean showing a lot more humanity and heart than grit and discipline.

But you can never accurately replicate what it's like to serve an actual prison sentence. So, as part of my managerial training, I volunteered to spend some time inside one of the most unusual jails in the world.

It's not in the UK and for legal reasons I can't say precisely where it is, except that it's part of an experiment to find out how inmates should best be treated, so they can make a life for themselves after they're released. This prison is located in a huge faux mansion in the grounds of a top security women's jail in the middle of a deserted forest 50 miles from the nearest town.

Few people know it even exists because only a dozen inmates live there at any one time and they're obliged to sign a confidentiality agreement to never speak publicly about it. Its very existence could cause a storm of controversy if news of it ever leaked out in the media. The dozen or so women living inside this mansion when I arrive are nearly all convicted murderers. And they're not even necessarily in the final stages of their sentences, either.

Many politicians across the world would be up in arms if they realised these specially selected convicts are free to wander the entire building and its surrounding gardens without full supervision. And, to make matters worse, there is only ever *one* guard on duty inside the mansion. The idea behind it all is to entrust these inmates with an unprecedented amount of freedom and then to see how they respond.

I spent a week as an officer inside this small prison, working for up to 12 hours each day. It ended up teaching me more about the psychology of prisons and the way that inmates should be treated than probably anything else I've ever done in my entire career. Inside this prison, the female inmates cooked me meals, talked to me about their lives and intelligently analysed many aspects of their incarceration. And all of them agreed that at the end of the day, having these extra freedoms inside gave them a new lease of life.

One of them told me: "In a normal prison you're treated like a child. No one trusts you to even go to the shower alone. It's humiliating and repressive and in the end you either get resentful or beaten down. Your confidence goes and when you do finally get out, you're not really mentally able to cope with it.

"You turn into a zombie, afraid to do anything in case you get dragged back to prison, but it's impossible to survive in that type of mental state in the outside world. You end up returning to your old habits and then you're slung back inside."

There were many aspects of life inside this mansion that were ground-breaking but the most remarkable of all was that, unlike most other prisons, drugs were non-existent. Obviously, it's easier to control the consumption of drugs in a small building occupied by a dozen inmates, instead of hundreds, if not sometimes thousands. But the lack of drugs inside this mansion had been achieved without any body searches or restrictions of any sort. There was simply no demand for them.

One inmate explained: "You don't need drugs in here because it's not a repressive place like a normal jail. People only use drugs inside prison to escape the hopelessness of their situation. We like it in here."

The female inmates were allowed twice-weekly visits from their loved ones, too. And once a month, the children of inmates under the age of 10 were permitted to stay overnight in specially decorated bedrooms with their mothers.

My visit to the mansion forced me to completely rethink the prison system in the UK. If such a place was opened up in this country, it could be used to re-educate and re-enthuse both male and female inmates. Who knows? Eventually maybe all prisons could be run this way and then the prison population would undoubtedly shrink, which would save taxpayers a fortune.

My memories of that prison within a prison have always stayed with me and helped make me doubly determined to try and improve the UK's often backward prison system. I realised the key was to ensure that prisons altered the perception of what most people thought of them. The extreme opinions of offenders are there for all of us to see and hear. It often feels as if those in prison will never completely unshackle the prejudices that society inflicts on them. The public needs to realise that prisoners are worth investing time and money in.

Remember those teachers some of us had at school, who actually took the time to help us understand and appreciate subjects? Similarly, prison staff need to be prepared to show inmates more patience and understanding than bland indifference.

* * *

My first managerial job on that long ladder towards becoming a prison governor was as a line manager on the wing of one of the UK's toughest prisons. Line manager is a strangely detached job in many ways – the exact opposite of being out in the field, which I'd enjoyed for so much of my career up to this time. Now I was tasked with organising a team of 12 wing POs by carefully organising and managing their schedules and duties to ensure their efficiency on the job.

It was the first time I'd ever stepped back and taken a proper look at the system that I was so convinced I could change. I quickly appreciated that it was going to be a lot harder to achieve this goal than I thought when I was a younger, ideal-istic PO. Juggling the schedules of 12 hard-working POs in order to help keep them and the inmates reasonably content (and safe) was akin to juggling 12 plates in the air without letting any of them smash to pieces on the ground.

As line manager, I was expected to implement and monitor all the systems on a prison wing, including everything from work shift rotas to making sure the prisoners were safely tucked up in the correct cells at the end of each day. I also had to help coach those staff members to ensure they abided by all ethical and other sensitivity rules at all times. A lot of this was aimed at trying to dismantle much of the racism and bullying by staff, which I'd seen so much of as a young PO.

The trouble was that a lot of closed-off prison officers go through the motions when it comes to these topics. It was frustrating because I wanted to improve things virtu-ally overnight but I had to quickly adjust my expectation levels accordingly. The hardest part of being a line manager, though, was to regularly issue operational instructions and talk through emergency procedures with my POs. Many officers under me were considerably older and seemed to look on me as a young upstart.

So initially, it felt like I was tearing my hair out as a line manager. But I learned to appreciate this was all part of the promotional system. Because at the end of the day, everything – good and bad – that those 12 POs did under my manage-ment was my responsibility. Being a line manager also helped me to appreciate the complexities of running a prison, which is something most POs rarely even think about during their career. The management training system was – and still is – supposed to prepare you for all eventualities but I soon found out this certainly wasn't the case.

CHAPTER 19
DAMAGED

There are a handful of prison inmates in the UK who didn't start off as lifers but then committed crimes behind bars, which ended up costing them their liberty for decades. One psychiatrist I know told me once that a lot of these inmates were very child-like characters and each time they caused trouble it felt incredibly close to a baby throwing a tantrum.

There's no doubt that many of them went through difficult childhoods. These left such huge scars on their characters and stunted their emotional growth. But that is no excuse for what some of them ended up doing.

One such prisoner was so notorious inside a number of prisons that I can't even give him a nickname without risking making him recognisable. A lot of the time, he'd apparently seemed a jovial enough character and could even be extremely popular with other inmates, as long as he always got his own way. But when he didn't, he became extremely violent. And on those occasions, it would take at least four burly POs to contain him. He'd usually end up being dragged into the seg unit to cool off. But these types of incidents had been happening to him for the best part of 20 years.

His original crimes had carried a five-year prison sentence, but he'd broken the law so many times in prison that many predicted he'd never actually be released. Most incidents ended up with him injuring POs, as well as inflicting damage on any inmates who got in the way. He'd then find himself hauled into the governor's office to face yet more charges, which he usually pleaded guilty to.

My very first encounter with this inmate occurred just after I'd been promoted to wing governor at one of the UK's most infamous top security prisons. I was back in the thick of it after mainly pushing pens and planning work schedules as a line manager.

As wing governor, I was expected to make all the day-to-day proactive decisions on that wing, from dealing with inmates' suicide attempts to faulty toilet systems. Being wing governor also gave me the time to deal with inmates individually, which enabled me to try and work out the best way to handle each one, while at the same time improving the general atmosphere on the wing.

All this made the wing's most troublesome inmate a perfect 'guinea pig' for me to study closely. At that time, this prisoner remained locked down in the seg unit and wasn't even allowed out for meals as he'd recently kidnapped a member of staff and held him hostage for what seemed like no apparent reason.

The officer snatched during that incident had been rescued by the prison's rapid deployment squad following a nine-hour stand-off. Most staff did believe, though, that this inmate hadn't intended to ever actually harm anyone and just did it all out of frustration. But that didn't preclude him from being punished, which included not being allowed to leave his cell on the seg unit.

Despite being wing governor, I decided to personally serve him breakfast, lunch and dinner on the seg unit. The POs were bemused when I explained to them that I felt getting to know him properly was a priority, especially since he was scheduled to return to the main wing within a few weeks. I, not for the first time, believed there was some wisdom in my unconventional work methods, although I knew there was little point in trying to convince the staff about any of this, until I'd proved my point.

So it was with some trepidation that I began my first morning at that prison by delivering this inmate's breakfast pack through the flap in the cell door where he was locked up for the time being. Moments after I pulled down the flap on his cell door, a wide-open mouth pressed so close over the opening that all I could see was a full-on view of his swollen tonsils.

He insisted I pushed the breakfast pack through the flap and he'd take it with what few teeth he still had. I played along with him after one senior PO had told me earlier it was always better to humour him at first, otherwise he'd turn 'psycho'.

After he'd taken the pack, I closed the flap. On the other side of the door, he screamed that I'd smashed him on the nose. I could tell it was an elaborate trick, just designed to re-engage me in more conversation, as his face hadn't been anywhere near the flap when it closed.

I played along with him, opening it again and trying to sound sympathetic while apologising for closing it on his face. He laughed and said he was only kidding around. I gently shut the flap and headed off to the next cell.

As I walked away, I heard a barking sound coming from his cell. This was quickly followed by a howling noise like a wolf out on the prairie. I decided it was probably best to ignore him, although many of the other inmates in their cells were so amused by his antics that they shouted encouragement for him to continue.

When I asked one PO why he made such a performance of everything, he replied: "He's sizing you up to see if you're worth snatching, guv. Don't be fooled by the 'I am a nutter' routine." All the other POs on the seg wing said that as long as he was in solitary, we were all safe. But he was due out of seg in a couple more weeks and I remained determined to get to the root causes behind his disruptive behaviour.

So, against the advice of many of my POs, I continued delivering those meal packs to his cell in order to try and establish proper lines of communication with him. Gradually, he began unravelling parts of his life to me, including how he'd been abused by a teacher at his school and decided to burgle the man's home in revenge. That had set him off on the path to crime.

He also disclosed how he'd ended up in a borstal alongside his older brother, who'd been murdered in front of his very eyes during a fight in the yard. I didn't know if he was telling me the truth, but he was close to tears as he spoke, so I felt like I should believe him. He said seeing his own brother being murdered had destroyed his spirit, as well as his trust in people, particularly after the governor at the borstal refused to properly investigate the murder and so the killers were never even prosecuted.

After spending a couple of weeks talking to him, the governor of the prison confirmed his release back on to the wing from the seg unit. A lot of the POs warned me never to forget about this inmate's previous behaviour, and I did make sure to keep what I knew he was capable of in the back of my mind.

Despite those ominous predictions from staff, though, he steered clear of trouble for the following six months, after which I was transferred to work as wing governor at another prison. Before I left, he even gave me a photograph from the 1930s that featured a prison officer being held up with a gun by a prisoner.

"Don't worry, guv. It's not you," he said, smiling, as I read it. The prison officer in the photo was fat and red-headed and actually resembled one of the most hated officers on the wing.

As I left that prison for the last time the following day, I had a sneaking suspicion it wouldn't be the last time I would come across that man.

* * *

Less than a year later, that same inmate held three other prisoners hostage and threatened to behead them if he wasn't given a better cell. With the prison's rapid response unit on standby to rescue the prisoners, he insisted he'd only negotiate through me for the release of his hostages.

I was abroad on holiday at the time and no one contacted me. If I'd known what was happening, I would have come straight back to try and help. Instead, a senior prison service negotiator attempted to talk him into surrendering. Unfortunately, it ended badly when he sliced the finger off one inmate before being overpowered by a rapid response unit.

He got another 10 years on his sentence for that. Afterwards, I remembered something he'd told me when we'd met before.

"I really don't give a shit what people think of me," he said. "I'm not out to scare folk. I suppose a lot of my problems are down to boredom and an overwhelming feeling that life dealt me a bad card in the first place." The idea goes that if his childhood trauma had not occurred, he probably would have ended up having a happy and productive life. But tragically, it was not to be.

However grim the whole affair may have been, it had re-emphasised to me how important it was that the prison system considered these types of mitigating circumstances about a prisoner's background, because that might then change the way we deal with them. And that, in turn, could help reduce the number of inmates coming in and out of prison on a regular basis.

I hoped that one day I might be able to try and put this and other ideas into action, but there was still a long way to go before I could really make a difference.

CHAPTER 20
MOB JUSTICE

Paedophiles are considered dirt by virtually everyone inside prison. That makes them at risk from the moment they arrive in the reception area. And it's not just the prisoners you have to worry about. It's hard trying to convince a PO on the ground to be fair when dealing with these offenders, as they're understandably perceived to be contemptible human beings.

All this doesn't make the problem of accommodating child sex offenders in a prison any easier. You can't just throw them in a seg unit and forget about them because, if at all possible, they should be properly integrated into the prison system.

I was in my late thirties and had just been promoted to deputy governor at a women's prison. It was the last, but biggest, rung in the promotional ladder to becoming a governor, so it was crucial I made a good impression. I soon discovered in that jail there was just as much anger towards paedophiles from female inmates, especially those with children of their own.

I'd worked in female prisons as a wing governor and PO before but this time I was number two in the entire jail, which meant being on call at all times of the day and night in order to deal with every aspect of the running of that prison. As the number two, I was expected to be the governor's eyes and ears on the ground. However, that also meant learning not to trouble him with the more mundane aspects of prison life. It was an excellent way to learn the main administrative ropes of running a prison, though.

In that prison, I came across one of the few female sex offenders I ever encountered. She was a middle-aged woman who'd been found guilty of abusing her own niece. She arrived with a batch of other inmates one hot summer's day. Her case had been given massive press coverage, especially in the tabloids who'd labelled her 'The Aunt from Hell'.

On the surface, she seemed no different from most other child sex offenders – mainly men – whom I'd come across during my prison service career. They tended to be loners, who didn't look others in the eye and usually appeared extremely shy.

There was an additional complication when it came to this inmate, though; she hadn't been named in court to protect the identity of her niece. The prison service warned us in advance that it would be impossible to hide her identity once the prison rumour mill started up, so we had to remain extra vigilant and not assume that her current anonymity would protect her. And somehow, within hours of her arrival at the prison, most of the inmates knew she was the so-called 'aunt from hell'. I suspected that some of the POs had helped spread the rumours, as they were all so evidently disgusted by the case.

I was deeply troubled by the way some staff had taken it upon themselves to be judge, jury and executioner of this inmate, whatever her offence. Prison officers are supposed to be impartial at all times. But I chose not to confront any of my staff because I had no actual proof, other than my suspicions, about their behaviour. I also knew the prison would fall apart if I ripped into any staff members, especially without sufficient substantiation to back up my accusations.

For the first time since being promoted from PO, I wasn't certain I could trust my own staff members to protect an inmate, despite my orders. The main issue to deal with, though, was who would agree to share a cell with this supposed paedophile. In male prisons, most paedophiles are housed in a Vulnerable Prisoner Unit (VPU) more commonly known as the 'numbers' or 'beast wing' where inmates are kept away from the main prison population for their own safety.

Because the number of female paedophiles is relatively low, there are rarely such facilities available to keep them in separate wings in female jails, so they have to stay with the general population. And getting someone to share a cell with a paedophile is not easy. Most inmates don't want to for obvious reasons and you certainly can't put similar offenders together in cells.

Psychiatrists have warned for decades that if you put two paedophiles in a cell together then they're likely to 'team up' and begin plotting together, or at least enabling behaviour. This could make them more dangerous once they're released.

The governor ordered that our sex offender should be moved from cell to cell on fortnightly cycles, until she ended up with someone who was prepared to accept her long term. On her first full day on my wing, glass was put in her food in the canteen and every single inmate there refused to even acknowledge her, let alone talk to her.

The twist was that this supposed 'evil sex fiend' – as the tabloids had also labelled her – was actually a softly spoken university lecturer whose own children insisted publicly she was innocent of all the allegations. Her case centred on a weekend when she looked after her sister's two children while her sister went on holiday with her new boyfriend. On her return, the sister had interrogated her children – who were aged five and seven – about their weekend and they inferred that their aunt and uncle had 'hurt' them.

Without any further investigation, the mother had accused her own sister and her husband of abusing the two children while she was away. She'd reported all this to the police and the children had been examined by physicians who found marks and bruises on both children that appeared to be consistent with the abuse allegations.

Shortly afterwards, the sister and her husband were arrested by police on child sex charges. The aunt was distraught about the allegations. She and her husband even went through the humiliation of a lie detector test to try and convince the police they were innocent. The aunt failed the test while her husband passed, so police dropped the charges against him. They still went through with the prosecution of his wife, even though lie detector tests are not admissible in a UK court of law due to reliability issues.

In the end, the aunt pleaded guilty but only to a lesser charge of causing physical harm to the two children. She claimed both of them had fallen off their bicycles when she took them out to the park, and this was how the bruises occurred.

The two-year jail sentence the aunt received was considered harsh, especially as the alleged sex offences were never proven. It had seemed like a trial by media and one tabloid had even paid the mother of the two children thousands of pounds for an interview, in which she labelled her own sister as a paedophile.

Not surprisingly, the so-called 'aunt from hell' looked like a broken woman by the time she arrived in the prison where I was deputy governor. Her head was bowed most of the time and she seemed terrified of everyone. She was often found sobbing in her cell, even during recreation breaks when she should have been in the yard with the other inmates.

She told staff she was afraid to go in the yard with other inmates because a number of them had threatened to kill her. I was so concerned about her safety that I asked her if she wanted to be transferred to a single cell in the prison's small seg unit. She refused, saying that she believed people would presume she was guilty if she asked to be isolated.

I respected her decision but there was also her ill mental health to consider, as well as tackling those perceived threats against her life. So instead I ordered the officers on her wing to keep a close eye on her and this time I warned each of them in turn that they had to put their feelings to one side about her, although I still noticed some of them sneering whenever her name was mentioned.

Meanwhile, this inmate's husband and children regularly came to see her. They were clearly heartbroken and tended to suffer greatly in the visiting area, as most other families spent the entire time glaring at them.

One PO heard another inmate on the wing warning this woman that if she was seen hugging or showing any affection towards her family in the visitor area, she'd be attacked on the wing because other prisoners' families didn't want to see that. When I heard about it, I asked the wing staff to warn the PO to make sure that the next time she heard such threats, the inmate concerned should be put up on charges. I feared the POs wouldn't bother because they seemed to hate that inmate as much as the other prisoners did.

Not being able to hug your own family or explain why you couldn't would be disturbing for anyone, let alone a deeply depressed inmate who insisted she'd been wrongly convicted. None of the other inmates or staff even contemplated that she might be innocent. They just assumed she was ashamed of the crime she'd committed, and thus hated her for it.

When she issued some pleas of innocence and appeals of sympathy to the media through her lawyer, inside the prison this had the opposite effect of simply fuelling further resentment against her. Eventually her own family contacted me directly to ask about her mental health. She'd asked them not to visit her anymore because she felt it was too distressing for them. I began to worry myself as I could tell those threats from other inmates were terrifying her.

Many of the inmates in neighbouring cells continued to taunt her. Some would bang on her cell door to disturb her and at night inmates shouted abuse at her from inside their cells. On the rare occasions when she came out of her cell, inmates would spit on her in the corridor. Not surprisingly, she was soon considered a suicide risk and while this would normally be solved by putting her on constant watch, I couldn't even be certain the staff would regularly monitor her to make sure she was okay.

One time, I was doing a wing tour following a visitor session and I found her sobbing on her bed, while all the other inmates were out in the yard. She said she was afraid to even talk to me in case any of the other inmates or staff found out. She seemed very close to at the very least harming herself.

I held a meeting of POs later that day in the wing office and demanded that they check on her wellbeing through the door flap every five minutes. Only a few of them even bothered to nod their heads. It was my duty as deputy governor to try and work out how to help this woman and somehow disperse all the anger being directed at her.

A lot of people asked why I cared so much, given she'd been convicted of harming a child. But by this time, I'd closely studied the reports of her case and realised her guilt wasn't as cut and dried as the media had made out. There were huge question marks about the honesty of her sister and a long history of problems between them.

This went all the way back to when they were children and a relative had been rumoured to have abused the sister. Nothing ended up happening there, but I felt like, whatever the truth, some scars would remain. In any case, whether guilty or not, our prisoner's jail sentence had turned into a form of abuse in itself.

The following day, one of the senior wing officers reported that the inmate was refusing to leave her cell, even at mealtimes. The previous night someone had left a cardboard box filled with excrement outside her door. I asked the governor for permission to transfer her to the seg unit so that she could be kept in solitary for her own protection. He refused because she hadn't asked for a transfer herself.

So I went back to see her to try and explain that she needed to be the one to request a move. But she wouldn't even talk to me. She'd completely retreated into her own shell and was sitting on her bed curled up in a ball rocking back and forth. I should have asked the governor to call in mental health experts at that point. Just before I left the cell, I told her I was going to recommend that, but she asked me not to do it and assured me she would be okay.

Two days later, two POs found her trying to hang herself from the bars of her cell window. Her latest cellmate had insisted on being transferred after claiming that the woman had scared her by threatening to kill her.

After her failed suicide attempt, the inmate was taken by stretcher to an in-patient section on the other side of the prison. As she was being moved, the other prisoners jeered and shouted that it was a shame she hadn't managed to kill herself.

Once in the medical ward she was examined by a health-care team, who decided it wasn't necessary for her to be taken to hospital, which meant going back to the wing. In the end, we were able to put her in a single cell in the seg unit when she was ready to leave the infirmary. To make matters worse, her suicide attempt was splashed all over the tabloids two days later. I had little doubt someone on the prison staff had tipped them off. Everyone had such a dislike for her, though, that it could have been anyone.

Many of the female inmates openly boasted that they'd driven her to attempt suicide. And most POs continued to do nothing about the backlash against this woman. Some were even annoyed she'd been put in the seg unit. This time I admonished some of the most opinionated POs and told them I'd take action to at least get them re-educated if they didn't step up to the programme and perform their duties in a fair and balanced manner.

That woman inmate's heartbroken husband then gave an interview to a TV station. He talked about a feud between the two sisters which he said lay behind the accusations that were made against them both when they looked after the two children. The interview with the husband had little impact because most of the public had already decided his wife was guilty and her suicide attempt only seemed to further confirm that in their minds.

About a week after all this, I was called down to the main common area of the wing after two women had tried to shiv each other following an argument about what to watch on the television. One of them was the sex offender's former cellmate.

Two POs who broke up the fight told me she'd kept saying to the other woman: "I know what you did, you fuckin' bitch." She refused to explain what she meant and the other inmate kept calling her a 'fuckin' grass'.

In the end, I ordered them both to be put in the seg unit to cool off. I also asked two of the senior POs if they knew what the women were arguing about. They both looked awkwardly at each other and said they had no idea, even though it was obvious they were lying. I warned them that if I wasn't told the full story about what had happened, then heads would roll.

The following morning, the same two POs sheepishly informed me that the sex offender's former cellmate had told them that she'd been forced by another inmate to leave the cell earlier on the day that inmate had tried to kill herself, so that two female prisoners could then 'persuade' her to commit suicide.

The inmate said she was coming clean about what had happened in the hope she'd get her time in prison reduced. This type of information is often fabricated in an attempt to get an early release, so these things tend not to be paid attention to. And, with no evidence to back up her claims, I had no choice but to ignore them, but I did have suspicions that they had a ring of truth to them. It was entirely likely that certain POs hadn't bothered to monitor that inmate on the night she tried to hang herself, and that they still believed she deserved to die for what she'd supposedly done to those two small children.

I examined all the relevant CCTV images to see if I could see any evidence that backed up her cellmate's allegations. I eventually came across footage of a PO unlocking the cell shortly before two inmates entered it. They came out less than five minutes later. Soon after that, the woman had tried to hang herself. Although the footage itself didn't prove what had actually happened, it definitely looked as if she'd been coerced into trying to commit suicide.

If I revealed my suspicions to her family, it might be even more upsetting for them, so I decided to keep that to myself. I did manage, though, to get the inmate transferred to a special mental health unit, where she could at least be properly looked after.

A month later, the case yet again exploded on to the front pages of the tabloids and the TV news when the mother of the abused children was secretly recorded saying to a relative that she knew her sister was innocent. She'd said she felt bad about dumping her children and sleeping with her lover, who'd that day refused to leave his wife for her, which is why she was particularly angry.

It seemed that this poor woman had been innocent all along. The woman herself was eventually released on appeal following her sister's confession, but her family said her mental health had been damaged for life by her experiences in prison. The mother of the children never paid the price for ruining her sister's life because the aunt refused to give evidence against her sister.

Not long afterwards, I heard that she'd been diagnosed with early onset of Alzheimer's. She and her husband had moved to the countryside to get away from the stigma attached to the case. Doctors were quoted in one newspaper as saying that the Alzheimer's was almost certainly caused by the stress she suffered due to her conviction and subsequent term in prison.

The twists and turns of this tragic case showed that a prisoner's conviction should not be allowed to influence the way they're treated in prison if at all possible. It's a tricky balancing act, though, because no prison system could operate effectively if an inmate's offence was kept entirely secret from staff and other inmates. I thought I knew all the answers but this case proved a definite wake-up call.

* * *

Shortly after that unfortunate woman inmate departed the prison where I was serving as deputy, I was informed that I was on a shortlist of three to become a prison governor for the first time. I attended an interview with the service board, which was supposed to rubber-stamp my suitability for the job. However, I sensed from the moment I sat down in front of the panel that a couple of them were waiting to catch me out.

The same ones also seemed bothered by my lack of academic qualifications but I tried not to let any of this get to me.

I was worried, though, that if I behaved in a detached manner then that might give them the impression I was arrogant and blasé. I needed to reassure them about my management skills without making them think I was some kind of cold fish. So I told them that once I became a governor, I'd do everything in my power to encourage inmates to feel that their safety was my top priority while at the same time maintaining prison discipline. A couple of panel members nodded but no one uttered a word in response.

Then one old gent asked me if I believed in the death penalty. I noticed a couple of younger prison officials take a sharp intake of breath in anticipation of how I was going to respond. I hesitated because it was the one question I hadn't prepped for.

"Under no circumstances should the death penalty be reintroduced," I said. That was it. I let my words hang in the air for them all to absorb, convinced I'd just cost myself my first governor's post.

Moments later, I was told the interview was over and that they "would be in touch soon". I left the room totally deflated. I was certain I'd blown it and went straight home and got drunk with my partner, who worked as a PO. It was a relief to talk to someone who truly appreciated what the job entailed.

Early next morning, I was having a rare lie-in when the phone rang. I was so groggy from my hangover that I didn't know what to say at first when I heard the secretary from the prison service asking if it was me. After my reluctant reply, she curtly informed me I was officially in line to take over the next available governor's position after being approved by the prison service board. I thought I was hearing things at first. It only sunk in when she added that I'd be informed of my first posting in due course.

That first prison as a governor, though, would present me with some very different problems from the ones that panel no doubt thought were so important.

CHAPTER 21
DEADLY GROUND

My first prison as chief was a relatively new jail housing female inmates, most of whom were considered to be a high security risk. These prisoners included female drug dealers, gang bosses, murderesses and the wives of much more notorious professional criminals who'd been prosecuted for committing crimes on behalf of their husbands.

One of the prisoners in this jail's seg unit was a Libyan woman who'd been found guilty of carrying out three contract killings on behalf of one of London's most powerful crime families. This woman had arrived in the UK as a teenager 20 years earlier when her parents had escaped the tyrannical regime of Libyan dictator Colonel Gaddafi.

She was remarkably open about her crimes, even boasting to one female officer that each time she killed a man it made her feel liberated as she'd been raped by a gang of men in Tripoli when she was 13. This Libyan inmate had a girl-friend inside the main prison area but she'd ended up in the seg unit after a fight with another woman in the yard. When she was being moved, she'd been furious because she wanted to be with her lover.

In my experience, staff and inmates inside women's prisons have always seemed to take a more pragmatic attitude towards gay relationships behind bars. Many women have told me down the years it's often more about companionship than sex. A lot of them have been badly treated by men in the past, so they trusted women more, and this trust bred intimacy.

A few days after the hitwoman had been put in the seg unit, two senior police detectives came to see me as they believed she'd been paid by the same gang she used to work for in London to kill the wife of one of her old bosses, who was being held in the same jail. The police alleged that the gang leader feared that his wife was about to reveal all their secrets to the police in exchange for her own freedom and he'd commissioned the hit on her to guarantee her silence.

However, the police admitted they couldn't prosecute the Libyan woman or the gang boss unless they caught her in the act of trying to kill the wife, as everything they knew at that stage was just hearsay. So the police requested that I let the Libyan woman back on to the main wing from the seg unit so she could be monitored and hopefully caught as she prepared to carry out the killing. And the police insisted the wife shouldn't be told she was on a hit list in case she confronted her husband about it.

The entire operation was incredibly risky. It placed me, as a new governor, right in the firing line. There was a risk that the crime boss's wife might end up being killed if my staff didn't intervene fast enough, and if that happened I'd be in trouble. After much soul-searching about the proposal, I refused to cooperate and suggested the Libyan woman was transferred to another prison. I felt I couldn't just stand by and encourage a murder to take place in my prison.

Despite my resistance, the police went over my head and pressured the prison service, and I was ordered to still release the Libyan woman back on to the main wing from the seg unit. I hated doing it, although really I had little choice in the matter. The crime boss's wife was a sitting duck and it was all happening inside the first prison I'd ever run.

Behind the scenes, I tried to force through a transfer for the gangster's wife to another prison on the grounds that she and other prisoners and staff were at risk if the hit went ahead inside my prison. I knew it would infuriate the police, so I didn't inform them. At first the prison service seemed extremely reluctant to back me up, particularly as they had agreed with the police's plan initially. It would be a huge gamble defying the police but I was determined to show my bosses how seriously I took my job as a governor.

After much wrangling, the prison service eventually agreed, albeit reluctantly, to back up my request and over-ruled the police's plans. Although I got my wish, I was told the transfer couldn't go ahead for another two weeks because of a shortage of space at all the prisons where the gangster's wife could possibly be sent. And now I couldn't even get the Libyan woman returned to the seg unit because that was also full, so I ordered my POs to monitor the mobster's wife round the clock, especially when she wasn't in her cell.

The first few days of this period of waiting went off without any incidents, but just knowing the Libyan hitwoman was on the same wing as her target put me on edge. In the middle of all this, wing staff reported to me that the crime boss's wife had started becoming very aggressive towards the Libyan inmate. I presumed she'd found out her husband had hired her to kill her, and that this had caused her agitation. But actually the wife had discovered the Libyan woman had been having an affair with her husband before she went to jail. Little did she know this was the least of her problems.

All this gave me the perfect excuse to speed up the transfer process and the police didn't discover we'd finally moved the gang boss's wife until a few hours after she'd left the prison. They were incensed, but I believed I'd just done my own career a lot of good by standing up to them. And, more importantly, I'd prevented a murder and most likely a lot of collateral damage as there is always a risk to the staff and inmates in general when these things happen.

The Libyan woman did end up doing a deal with the police but was murdered by another inmate in a different prison less than a year later. Many inside the prison service believe she may herself have been targeted by the same gang, who'd hired her to kill that mobster's wife.

I guess what goes around...

CHAPTER 22
OFF MESSAGE

Even by the time I began working as a full-time governor, the aftermath of 9/11 – more than half a dozen years earlier – continued to be linked to religious fanaticism inside UK prisons. My first men's prison as governor contained Muslim gangs inside the two main wings. They'd congregate together at mealtimes in the canteen and in the yard. A 'them and us' atmosphere existed between the Muslim prisoners and the rest of the prison population. Many other inmates referred to them as terrorists behind their backs, even though a lot of the Muslim inmates were in prison for offences unrelated to terrorism and had no involvement with such activities.

Running an entire prison meant I had much less opportunity for direct contact with prisoners compared to when I was a PO. But I tried to make a point of speaking to as many inmates as possible, and in this prison I wanted to make a special effort to meet members of the radical Islamist gangs. However, they didn't respond well to approaches by me and the staff most of the time. They seemed to relish their fearsome reputations, which they openly boasted was a form of 'payback' after years of being ignored in most prisons before the nightmare of 9/11 occurred.

Also, by this time – all those years after 9/11 – supposedly radical inmates were converting younger, more impressionable prisoners into becoming practising Muslims. The younger inmates seemed to be looking for a 'family' to belong to, although I fully accept that others were genuinely interested in the religion itself, as they had every right to be. My staff insisted that some of these 'conversions' were not connected in any way to religious beliefs but to the higher quality of food that the prison service was obliged to supply to members of the Muslim faith.

Around this time, the UK government of the day announced plans to train 30,000 extra police officers to help crack down on extremism. This was to include hundreds of specialist counter-terrorism staff, who'd make regular prison visits to speak to 'extremist' inmates. Many Muslim inmates convicted of terror offences eventually ended up spending months enrolled in such programmes, despite still being considered a threat by police and security services. There was even a push to increase the numbers of Muslim POs joining the service. Any ones that were recruited, though, were particularly hated by the more radical inmates.

* * *

From my limited personal experience as a prison governor, I'd already noticed that whenever a terror attack occurred anywhere in the world, it seemed to stir up hatred and violence between inmates, and caused a further deepening of the divide across races and religions. POs guarding offenders we considered 'extremist' often complained that they found themselves under almost constant threat from those inmates. Allegedly, one gang of Muslim inmates in the prison where I was now governor regularly warned guards that they would stream their beheadings on social media if they ever got a chance to kill them.

On one occasion, I received a tip from MI5 that a number of Muslim inmates in this same prison were planning to kidnap POs and kill them, unless they were provided with transport for an escape. It was alleged that these prisoners' associates on the outside were planning to launch a drone attack on the jail to aid the escape attempt. No such incident ever materialised but similar alleged threats from Muslim extremists were so numerous by this time that the UK security services began launching some high-risk operations to try and infiltrate terror cells.

Two MI5 agents turned up at the prison where I was governor to inform me that a convicted terrorist in residence was going to be given a new cellmate. They insisted it was 'a matter of national security' and revealed that this new cellmate was a Muslim man, whom I presumed worked for the security services. The plan was for him to gradually ingratiate himself with his terrorist cellmate, so that he'd eventually get recruited into the same group that this prisoner was affiliated to.

MI5 even planned that following his eventual 'release' from prison, their man would feed UK security services with inside information about any terror attacks that were in the pipeline. The two MI5 agents who visited my office to explain all this to me also insisted that I didn't tell my POs about their agent's real identity, to ensure his safety and the success of their operation.

I'd promised myself I would never deceive my staff, so this order left me feeling extremely conflicted. I considered trust to be the bedrock of everything inside prison. I tried to explain this to the two agents but they didn't seem to care and stated firmly that I had no choice in the matter.

I warned them that they could also be putting their undercover man at risk of attack from other convicted terrorists on the same wing, if their agent's real identity was uncovered. They insisted their man would be fine and repeated their assertion that I couldn't tell my staff anything. But when MI5 reluctantly handed over this new inmate's file to me to read, it left me even more doubtful about their reckless undercover operation.

This fake inmate wasn't just some fish out of water. He was a once idealistic young Asian university graduate who'd actually been on the verge of joining a couple of terror cells himself in the UK and Europe. He'd been arrested for an unrelated hit and run after knocking down a child with his car. The security services decided to 'turn him' and he'd agreed to work for them. His genuine arrest for that offence ensured that he'd appear to be a real prisoner, who was awaiting a proper trial.

Just a few hours after I'd met with the two MI5 agents, their 'spy' arrived at the prison to be processed in the reception area. He would eventually be transferred to the wing where he was to be put straight into a cell with the security services' target.

The entire operation seemed clumsy to me, particularly because it was quite unusual for a new inmate awaiting trial to be put straight into a convicted offender's cell. However, the agents insisted his cover would never be blown. All the while, I still wasn't allowed to tell my staff what he was actually doing in the prison and I continued feeling bad about lying to them. I was convinced their target would soon get suspicious about this stranger turning up in his cell. Later, I heard from one wing PO that both men had actually hit it off very quickly, so I decided to step back from the operation and stop fretting.

A few days later, MI5's undercover inmate became very aggressive with two of the wing POs after they refused to let him go to the Friday Muslim prayer session because he appeared to be intoxicated. A scuffle followed during which the undercover inmate tried to punch one of the POs. This would normally have been considered an automatic disciplinary offence so I immediately informed MI5 that their man would have to be transferred out of the cell he was sharing with their target as a result of the incident.

They insisted the incident had been deliberately engineered by their man in order to further convince the target that he was a genuine criminal and potential terrorist. They also claimed that my staff had been heavy-handed and provoked their man by being racist. MI5 wanted me to suspend one member of staff because that would provide him with a perfect alibi for not disciplining their man. Naturally, the POs on that wing were furious. They still had no idea who this new inmate really was and so naturally assumed I was just taking an inmate's side, which wasn't ideal.

A deputation of six officers came to see me to lodge a complaint about my decision not to charge the inmate. I tried to calm them down, although from our discussion they could tell something was going on. I feared that all the trust between us was on the verge of crumbling, and given I needed that trust to effectively run the prison, I told them the truth about the undercover operation.

I also asked them to respect my honesty with them by keeping what I'd said to them entirely confidential, and the wing POs reluctantly agreed to continue observing the terrorist and his undercover cellmate. However, I knew that if anything happened to either of them after I'd defied MI5 and told my staff the truth, then I'd probably be up on charges myself.

Within a few days, wing POs were reporting that six other Muslim inmates on the same wing had been deliberately avoiding the MI5 plant and his target during recreation time in the exercise yard and in the common area. While my staff were sure it was happening, they didn't know why. Then there was almost a fight between them all in the yard, and for the first time I found out that they'd all originally come from two rival drug gangs. The MI5 target and their undercover man had both been drug dealers before switching to terrorism.

I was furious that MI5 had not even bothered to mention these previous connections between their agent and target. When I confronted MI5 about this, they offered no apologies and insisted that I should let all the Muslims continue their battles on the wing, as they believed it would help their man to maintain his cover even more convincingly.

They also told me that two-man teams of MI5 officers would be visiting the prison once a week pretending to be defence lawyers so they could debrief their undercover cellmate. I had absolutely no doubt that this would mean their target and those other rival terrorists working out the real identity of their supposed undercover agent, but my protests fell on deaf ears.

During a visit to the wing a few days later, an older inmate approached me and asked to speak to me in private. I took him to the wing office where he explained to me that he'd been told that the six Muslim inmates were planning to take over one floor of the wing and then torture and kill the terrorist inmate and his MI5 cellmate. He said the Muslims and a number of other inmates on the wing were convinced the man in the cell with the terrorist was a plant. He told me that he'd heard it would all kick off within 48 hours.

I needed to come up with a solution very quickly. I couldn't transfer the inmate and the agent to other prisons without the permission of MI5, who'd already made it clear they wouldn't allow this to happen in the middle of their precious undercover operation. I asked my staff if they thought the old gangster's warning was believable and they said they had absolutely no doubt he was telling truth because the six inmates were almost constantly huddled together in the yard, which suggested they were planning something.

I realised then I needed a diversion in order to play for time, so I got my deputy governor to make an announcement over the prison's tannoy system that a bomb threat had been made against the wing. Then I phoned one of the MI5 agents to say I believed the bomb threat could be a diversion so that an escape could take place, but pointed out that it still had to be carefully checked out. He sounded irritated but he couldn't refuse to back me up on such a sensitive matter.

So all 200 of the inmates on the wing were herded into the yard while a search was carried out in every cell for 'bomb-making equipment'. A dog unit also came in to check every exposed area of the building where a 'bomb' itself might have been hidden.

Then, in the middle of this, a team of four MI5 officers turned up at the prison insisting that they needed to talk to their undercover agent. I explained that would be impossible until the yard lockdown ended and ordered them to stay in my office away from the wing while the bomb threat was being properly checked out. I believed this would give me time to activate a priority transfer order for the terrorist prisoner and his double agent cellmate so they could be moved to separate prisons. I didn't tell the MI5 agents what I was doing.

Still trapped inside my office, they became increasingly agitated as I continued to deny them access to the rest of the prison. Downstairs, their target and undercover man had been escorted from the yard through to the reception area and into separate sweat boxes so they could be driven to other prisons.

By the time I finally announced it was safe for MI5 officers to leave the prison, they'd gone. MI5 tried to get me fired for what I'd done. I pointed out that if those two inmates had stayed any longer in my prison there would have been a bloodbath.

Thankfully, the prison service backed me to the hilt and congratulated me on avoiding a nasty incident at the very least. I'd taken a huge gamble by defying the security services but luckily in the end, it actually helped rather than hindered my career. But by letting them use my prison to trap a terrorist, I'd put the lives of other inmates at risk. From now on, I would always maintain complete control of any prison I was running.

CHAPTER 23
AGAINST THE GRAIN

As a prison governor, I was expected to make constructive decisions in a boiling pot atmosphere and keep a lid on my own emotions. So at that second prison I ran, I went out of my way to try and placate both staff and inmates by relaxing some of the more antiquated rules inside that jail, some of which dated back to Victorian times.

The most insulting one of all was a petty regulation that all inmates had to shower together in shifts of at least 20 men because that enabled POs to monitor them more easily. Previous regimes at this particular prison had refused to change the rules to enable fewer prisoners to take showers at any one time. I not only overturned the rule but also had screens installed between showers to ensure inmates' reasonable privacy, as I believed this would significantly reduce violence and intimidation in the shower area.

But changing those rules in that prison prompted a derisory response from some staff members who complained that it made their jobs harder because they couldn't monitor the inmates as easily and that slowed up their duties. None of them appreciated the inmates' side in this argument, which was that the entire process was deeply humiliating.

Certain staff members were even more scathing after a deputation of prisoners sent me a note thanking me for what I'd done because my new rules meant showering was not anywhere near as traumatic as it had previously been. Those prisoners had been led by one extremely unusual inmate, known as AK. AK seemed refreshingly to contradict all the usual clichés of a manipulative and troublesome prisoner.

A lot of this was down to his background in the armed services, during which he was decorated for his bravery in two undercover army operations abroad that helped save the lives of many people. But during that final mission, AK had been shot in the left side of his head during a raid on an enemy stronghold and almost died. The bullet had gone clean through one side of his head and luckily for him it had missed his brain by millimetres. But AK's other injuries had left him with what he called 'a gammy left arm', which hung limply to his side.

Like so many who sacrificed themselves for their country, AK had ended up on the scrapheap in civvy street with a small pension and little else to show for 20 years of loyal service. Broke and addicted to prescription painkillers, he'd eventually been recruited by a crime gang, whose boss also happened to be AK's former brother-in-law. That's how he became an underworld killer, whose main job had been to wipe out any of the gang's enemies who dared to try and take them on.

By the time I encountered AK, he'd done a lot of time and had long since put his criminal past behind him. In fact, in prison he had become like a father figure to a lot of his fellow inmates, as most of them seemed to have the utmost respect for AK and often sought out his help on many issues. My predecessor at the prison had even left me a glowing report about AK, whom he described as being the heart and soul of his wing and someone who would actually help me to run the prison. This was an extraordinary accolade from a governor about an inmate.

Naturally, I was intrigued by this glowing report, so I made an effort to meet AK soon after starting my new job. He looked and behaved like a gentle grandfather type, with a grizzly grey beard, bright blue eyes and a voice so soft it was almost a whisper.

During that first meeting about the rule changes, I immediately began to understand the gravitational pull his gentleness had and actually found myself asking AK to stay behind so I could seek further advice on how to run my prison. And as I gradually mapped out my intentions, he seemed to nod his approval.

After I'd finished, he looked at me very intensely, squinted his eyes for a moment and then asked me very coolly why I'd even told him all this.

"I'm just another inmate. Nothing more," he said.

This disarmed me because I'd been expecting AK to be flattered by my attention. It dawned on me just how much I'd completely underestimated him. Not only was he wise, but incredibly humble too. After a few more minutes of awkward conversation, AK asked to be returned to his wing. Before he departed, he asked me to keep our discussion confidential as it would not help his credentials on the wing to be known as 'the governor's friend'. Back on the wing, the inmates continued giving him full respect and the majority of POs were equally careful in their interactions with him because they knew how much influence he had.

A few days after my meeting with AK, the wing POs reported that AK had actually talked a younger prisoner out of killing himself. When staff congratulated him, though, AK responded by saying he wasn't looking for gratitude because that young inmate shouldn't have felt that way in the first place. Of course, he was right. In a perfect world, we'd prevent all prison suicides, but it wasn't quite as simple as that. I knew there was no sense in pointing this out to AK but I kept wondering why he always felt the need to be on some crusade or other.

For the following few weeks, AK continually kept an eye on the younger prisoner to ensure he never felt like trying to commit suicide again. My staff reported to me that AK became obsessed with finding out why the younger prisoner had been driven to try and kill himself. AK began questioning other inmates on the wing, despite being warned by staff not to do so because they feared it would unsettle the prisoners.

Then a small deputation of POs came to me and asked me to order AK to halt his detective work as a number of inmates had been complaining that he was harassing them. Before I had a chance to call AK to my office for a reprimand, I received a staff report that the younger inmate who'd tried to commit suicide earlier had been found by POs in the showers armed with a shank.

He told staff he had the weapon for 'self-protection', but they suspected he planned to use it to attack another inmate. Then AK got involved. He asked the wing staff not to put the younger prisoner on a charge claiming there were 'mitigating circumstances', although he refused to say what they were.

AK was due to meet me anyway, so I waited for him to arrive rather than track him down. When he came to my office I told him that unless he told me the full story about why that young inmate was armed with a shank then that inmate would be severely disciplined.

AK hesitated for a few moments and studied me closely across the desk. It looked to me as if he was weighing up his next move. I repeated that unless I was told why that other younger inmate had the shank, I would have to charge him. AK then reluctantly told me that the younger inmate had been raped in the showers by another prisoner some months earlier before I'd taken over the prison. His attacker had been continually threatening to do it again, so the younger inmate felt he had no choice but to arm himself.

I discovered that the predatory inmate he named had twice been accused of similar attacks by other inmates during previous months, but he'd not been disciplined because neither of his victims were prepared to give evidence against him.

While I certainly couldn't condone any inmate being armed with a deadly weapon, I admitted to AK that I had a lot of sympathy for that younger inmate's predicament. I promised AK I'd get my staff to re-examine the other assaults said to have been carried out by the alleged sex attacker.

The following morning, the alleged predator asked one of the senior wing officers for protection saying that he believed that younger inmate was planning to kill him. He also insisted they'd had consensual sex and that the younger inmate had then become aggressive with him because he didn't want anyone to know he was gay.

Someone was about to be very seriously hurt or maybe even killed and it was my primary duty to prevent that happening, so I had to carefully think everything through. I wanted to make sure I didn't get the situation wrong, but I still wasn't absolutely sure who was telling the truth. And all the while, the tension on the wing was building as other inmates were openly pledging that they'd go after the alleged sexual predator prisoner themselves.

Believing he needed protection, the accused predator begged one of the senior wing officers to get him transferred to the seg unit. Later that same day, the accused was shanked in a corridor by AK. There were at least half a dozen witnesses but not one tried to stop the attack. The victim died of his wounds in hospital.

I went down to see AK in the seg unit immediately after the attack. He didn't deny what he'd done and said the younger inmate would have ruined his entire life if he'd gone through with the killing himself, so he'd done the deed himself instead. AK was almost 70 years old and said he didn't really care if he was never released from prison.

But it didn't all end there. The young inmate suffered a severe nervous breakdown and had to be transferred to a mental trauma hospital. He later told doctors he felt riddled with guilt because AK had killed the predator on his behalf.

AK was convicted of murder and given a further 12 years in prison. He was eventually transferred to the seg unit of another men's prison hundreds of miles away. During his trial he told the court he deeply regretted killing that inmate because he realised he should have forced him to make a full confession so that legitimate justice could have been served, rather than taking the law into his own hands.

Instead, the lives of three people had been irrevocably ruined. What a waste.

CHAPTER 24
THE HIT

Most governors arrive at work at the same time as a prison's civilian administrative staff. That's usually an hour after the main PO staff's early shift begins. But one morning I deliberately got in before the POs and ordered all of the staff from one wing to come to my office immediately. They didn't look too enthusiastic as they trooped in, but then this particular prison hadn't been very welcoming towards me since I'd instigated changes to the visiting rules, so that entire families – whatever the size – could visit an inmate at one time.

I also raised the bar regarding disciplinary action against inmates, so that they no longer faced time in the seg unit just for verbal outbursts against staff. The previous regime had, in my opinion, been using draconian rules to unfairly punish the inmates, often when they'd barely said a word to a PO.

That morning, I insisted all the wing staff sat down in my office – unusual in itself because these types of early morning gatherings usually only lasted a minute or two. Then I introduced them all to a police detective standing alongside me. He went on to explain to us that an informant had told the police that a contract had been taken out on the life of one of the wing's most notorious gangster inmates, the London-based head of the Russian mafia's Western European network.

The police believed that this inmate's bosses wanted to kill him to stop him telling any of their secrets in exchange for a lighter prison sentence. The officer insisted he had 'credible information' that an inmate on our wing was being paid to carry out the hit inside the prison. He told us he didn't know who that inmate was, but said there were at least a dozen possible 'contenders' serving their sentences on the same wing. They were all gangsters who'd been involved with drugs and money in the past.

It was clear that the police wanted to keep the Russian inmate alive because he was on the verge of cooperating with them. The POs and I told the detective that we were astounded he even considered it plausible that an unknown contract killer could strike inside our jail. He pointed out that there was an average of two murders every month inside UK's male prisons at that time, so maybe it wasn't so far-fetched.

Some POs present in my office immediately objected to the detective's tone. They thought he was implying that the POs might look the other way if the killer struck, which the detective apologised for as he hadn't meant the offence. However, he insisted the alleged hit was a real threat and we all needed to work together to try and prevent it happening.

He also asked us not to tell the target or any inmates about the so-called threat against him. When one PO said that surely the target had a right to know, the detective shook his head slowly and just said, "I'm afraid not." After he'd departed, I informed the staff that extra CCTV cameras were being installed throughout the wing in the hope this might deter the would-be killer from striking.

Having steeled ourselves for an attempt to murder that inmate, the wing was put on high alert. But for three or four weeks, absolutely nothing happened. Gradually, some staff began suggesting that perhaps this hit never existed in the first place.

Down on the wing itself, the Russian drug baron who was the apparent target had endeared himself to both the staff and inmates by turning out to be a very relaxed and charming character. He spoke openly about how he'd accepted he had to serve his sentence because it was part of his job. He even made a point of telling POs that his top priority was his family back in St Petersburg, Russia and making sure they were not put in any danger by his mafia bosses.

The police and my staff still had no idea who that killer on the wing really was, if he even existed. All the contenders originally suggested by the police did not really fit the bill. When the same detective asked me if any of my POs might be capable of doing it, I got even more protective about my staff and questioned whether the entire 'hit' was nothing more than a figment of the imagination of a bunch of paranoid coppers, after all. In spite of this suspicion, I still made sure the staff closest to me kept a very close eye on all the inmates and their fellow POs, just in case one of them gave away any clues that might lead us to the alleged killer in waiting.

On the wing itself, some of the sharper inmates began picking up a vibe that something was happening. The POs tried to ignore their questions but that seemed to make them even more unsettled. The atmosphere started to worsen when some inmates implied there had been a breakdown in trust between them and the staff.

While I was worrying about this growing tension on the wing, one morning a PO unlocked the door to the Russian's cell so he could come out for his breakfast pack. When there was no response, the officer entered the cell. He found the Russian lying slumped on the floor with a ligature around his neck, which was attached to the bars on the cell window.

Three officers arrived quickly on the scene and examined the body. They said the bruises around his neck clearly implied that he'd killed himself. The only other mark on his body was a scar where he'd had recent open-heart surgery. The prison doctor called to examine the Russian's body confirmed that he'd died of asphyxiation and proclaimed it was suicide. He was only 47 but he'd had a previous history of depression, so we felt it wasn't that surprising.

The police who arrived on the scene after the body was found were furious. They'd very much needed him to stay alive, which confirmed my belief they were either in the process of or at least trying to 'turn him' into an informant.

As with every sudden death in prison, though, the prison doctor could not officially confirm the cause of death himself. The Russian's body was taken to the local morgue to be examined by a pathologist. I was warned it might be at least 10 days before any examination could be completed, as their coroner was away on holiday at the time.

Back on the wing, and despite the lack of evidence to suggest it, rumours were spreading that the Russian had been murdered. A couple of the older inmates claimed to staff that they'd heard thudding sounds in the middle of the night when the Russian died and suggested someone had gone into his cell. But I was doubtful. How could anyone inside a top security prison have managed to enter a locked cell, kill a man and leave the cell without being seen, all in the middle of an overnight lockdown?

Less than two weeks later, the detective who'd originally brought his case to the prison called me. He sounded extremely irritated as he explained that within minutes of starting his examination of the Russian's body, the pathologist had recognised clear signs of fingermark bruises on his neck. It appeared he had been murdered after all.

That afternoon, a specialist forensics team turned up at the prison to examine the Russian's cell to see what clues could be found. Fortunately, it had been locked down since he died, so the crime scene remained pristine. All this external law enforcement activity was having an unsettling effect on a lot of the inmates on the wing, though. New rumours started that the Russian had been murdered by a renegade prison officer who'd been paid to carry out the hit by the cartel.

After the forensics team left the cell later that afternoon, the atmosphere on the wing got even worse as inmates became more aggressive towards staff members. Senior officers told me they feared that a further escalation of problems with inmates was inevitable.

So I ordered a complete lockdown until things had cooled. Some prisoners accused us of using bullying tactics on them by doing this, but I felt I had little choice in the matter. After all, a contract killing seemed to have been carried out inside my prison. This meant that no one could feel 100 per cent safe on the wing. And whoever it was, the killer was still on the loose. Some inmates continued to insist the contract killer was one of the POs, saying that was the only way the perpetrator could have got in and out of the cell.

Next morning, forensic examiners announced that the cell hadn't contained any evidence useful to the investigation. They believed the killer must have 'cleaned it' before leaving. This further implied it was an inside job and helped fuel even more wild rumours from the inmates.

The police pointed out that at the end of the day, whoever killed the Russian must have had access to his cell. This meant it could only have been a member of staff. Every inmate and staff member on the wing was interviewed by Scotland Yard investigators. After days of interviews, they came up with nothing.

Rumours that a prison officer carried out the killing were even published in the national newspapers. The main source was an inmate who'd been released from prison the previous morning. The media was excited because there was a touch of Agatha Christie about what had happened. How could someone murder an inmate inside prison and then disappear into thin air?

I feared that if I didn't find the killer then my career as a prison governor might soon be over as it had all happened on my watch and thus I would be held responsible. Fortunately, though, most of the public criticism was aimed at the police for not transferring the Russian to another prison or even telling him he was a target as soon as the original threat became known.

In the Press, there was further wild speculation that the killer had been a professional criminal inmate who'd been released shortly after the murder. But that was nothing more than pure speculation. Really, no one had anything to go on.

About three months after the murder, one of the most experienced POs on that wing retired. He was a popular figure with his colleagues and had a reputation for being charming to the inmates. A lot of my staff and I attended his leaving party in a pub close to the prison. We were all a bit surprised to see a couple of ex-inmates attending. One of them even stood up to make a very moving farewell speech for that officer.

No one commented specifically about the presence of those criminals, although I did notice some of the POs rolling their eyes when that ex-inmate gave his speech. All this reminded me that the retiring officer had been on duty the day the Russian had died, but he'd been cleared of involvement by the police after being interviewed.

Not long after retiring, he moved to southern Spain and lived in a large detached villa high up in the hills behind Marbella. Rumours drifted back to the prison that he was mixing with some shady underworld types on the nearby Costa del Crime, where many such characters had settled.

Shortly after that, the retired PO died in a street shooting incident in Marbella. Local police claimed he was caught in the crossfire between two warring Russian drug gangs. Upon hearing the news, many POs and police officers back in the UK said they thought it was a targeted killing.

Following the trail, one of the London tabloids tracked down his ex-wife and she admitted to them that he'd had money problems and she believed he had carried out the hit on the Russian in prison in exchange for £200,000. She also claimed to the paper that her ex-husband had become obsessed with security at his Spanish villa. She said that one of the Russian cartels wanted him dead in revenge for the murder of that Russian inmate.

The following morning, I double-checked the night- and day-shift records for the day of the original prison hit and noticed that one night-shift officer had gone off sick at the last minute but there was no record of who filled in for him. I contacted the night-shift wing governor and he remembered that the recently retired officer had volunteered at the last moment to do a double shift and work nights.

The police had earlier cleared him of involvement in the hit because they thought he'd only been on the day shift because the roster had not been altered when he volunteered to fill in on the night shift.

I'll never know for certain if that PO was involved in the Russian's murder, but it suddenly seemed much more likely. And all this had happened right under my nose. Once again, I felt responsible for the death of an inmate, even though the police had been publicly condemned because they'd refused to tell the Russian that he was a target.

I needed to take heed and try to make sure this never happened again on my watch.

CHAPTER 25
PRIME TARGET

The majority of disabled inmates – especially in my experience of men's prisons – tend to lie low, and keep themselves close to the POs in order to have any additional requirements met. It is an issue of contention for the administrators as they themselves, having had conversations with them first-hand, find themselves in a difficult position as they don't want to be seen by other inmates for favouritism.

However, when I was governor of one men's prison, I came across an inmate who, rather than having his disability prevent him from doing things, actually used his own circumstances to exert control over other prisoners. He was an Eastern European drug baron who'd been confined to a wheelchair after being shot by police during the raid that resulted in his arrest and subsequent conviction.

By the time I encountered him, he was already notorious within the prison service. He'd been regularly transferred between jails because he always gained considerable power and influence inside each prison where he was an inmate.

His prison file outlined how the previous governor had tried to tackle this inmate's activities by insisting only staff members were permitted to push his wheelchair around the prison. But then the POs' union stepped in and insisted that any POs escorting this disabled inmate should be paid danger money. They claimed this prisoner was a prime target for rival gangs inside the prison, whom he'd crossed inside the UK drugs underworld.

When the prison service turned down the union's demands for danger money, I knew I couldn't force the staff to be this inmate's carers without causing a huge rift between the prison management and the on-the-floor POs. Fortunately, I was able as governor to personally change some rules which were classified as internal and centred on just one prisoner. In the end, I reluctantly concluded that the only solution was to give three named inmates the responsibility of escorting the wheelchair prisoner around the wing.

Not surprisingly, the 'helpers' nominated by this inmate turned out to be three of his jailed henchmen who were suspected by staff of striking fear into many other prisoners on the wing. But this could never be proved because none of the victims would come forward to talk about the alleged intimidation. So I was left with no choice but to approve the applications by those three inmates.

It was my first big decision since taking over that prison and I knew it would upset many of the POs. However, I felt I had little choice but to allow this Eastern European to use these gangster inmates as his wheelchair helpers. I told my staff to warn them, though, that I'd transfer them to other jails if they became involved in any criminal activities inside my prison. And that also, if that happened, the disabled inmate would immediately be moved to the seg unit where prison staff would be obliged to look after him, which of course none of them wanted to do.

Within a few weeks of taking over this jail, my staff reported to me that the disabled inmate was running a drug and mobile phone 'business' on his wing. Unfortunately, when POs raided his cell, they didn't find any evidence of his criminal activities and he claimed he was being victimised because of his disability.

For the following few weeks, there was an uncomfortable stand-off between the prison staff and this disabled inmate (along with his henchmen) on the wing. Many senior staff accused me of not stamping down hard enough on their activities. But I needed to find concrete evidence of their crimes inside the prison and I believed the only way to do that was to lull the disabled inmate into thinking he'd scared us off by claiming we were harassing him.

While he was powerful, he didn't have all the inmates in his pocket. My POs informed me that six new prisoners who'd just moved on to the wing were members of an Asian street gang who hated his guts.

It turned out they'd bought drug shipments from the disabled inmate when they all operated in the underworld of the same city. Those young gangsters believed that the disabled criminal and his men had informed on them in exchange for shorter sentences, as they'd all been arrested in a coordinated series of raids by police SWAT teams.

I immediately contacted the prison service to request the transfer of the Asian gang members to other prisons to avoid a war on the wing. I was informed that the UK Justice Department wanted both gangs to remain on the same wing in the belief it would eventually scare some members of both gangs into becoming informants.

Naturally, I wasn't at all happy about this. It felt to me as if the prison service was being complicit in encouraging violence to occur on a wing, just to help the police. In the end, I kicked up such a stink that the service agreed that both gangs should be split up and transferred to other prisons to prevent that war kicking off inside my prison.

Tragically, overcrowding problems at other prisons were so severe at the time that none of them could be moved out of my jail for at least a month. I was well aware that it would be virtually impossible to protect those inmates 24/7, but it felt imperative we got through the month without any serious clashes between the two gangs.

For two and a half weeks an uneasy peace existed on the wing. There were a few minor skirmishes between the two gangs but nothing serious. Then one afternoon, the disabled inmate was sitting in his wheelchair watching a large TV set in the middle of the common area while most of his personal henchmen were out in the yard. Just one remained by his side.

On the screen, a World Cup qualifier football match between England and an Eastern European nation was about to kick off when members of the Asian gang drifted in from the yard. They soon began jeering at the TV screen from the top of a central stairway. When the disabled inmate glared up at them, they got even noisier and began insulting him by calling him a 'fuckin' cripple'. The disabled inmate sneered up at them and then gave them the finger, and that's when the Asian gangsters swarmed down the stairs towards him and his solitary henchman.

Only one guard was on duty in the common area at the time as the rest were in the yard. The lone officer found himself cut off from the nearest alarm button by two of the Asians blocking his way, while the four other gang members surrounded the disabled inmate and his one henchman.

Moments later, six staff members appeared in the common area and the Asian inmates immediately pulled away, leaving the Eastern European slumped forward in his wheelchair. Blood was spurting from a deep wound around his throat.

Two POs rushed to his side and started pushing the slumped inmate in his wheelchair towards the wing office at high speed. With constant jeers and taunts ringing out, the two POs swerved the wheelchair to avoid a table. It flipped over, throwing the disabled inmate on to the floor. As the officers struggled to drag his crumpled body back into the wheelchair, other inmates watched through the glass slits in their cell doors, laughing and applauding. They doubtless all hoped the disabled inmate was dead and seemed quite happy about it.

That murder actually had a huge calming effect on the wing because the victim had been such a divisive character. On reflection, I now realise the disability issue was secondary to the more basic elements at work here. A vicious gangster inmate had tried to control an entire prison wing. He was always going to be at risk, irrelevant of his physical condition.

Of course, I shouldn't have given those three hench-men tacit permission to escort him all over the prison. But more importantly, I should have known that if you lock up two sets of enemies on one wing, sooner or later everything will kick off.

CHAPTER 26
CANTEEN

In prison, if an inmate borrows anything from another inmate that automatically puts him or her in debt. It could be a tube of toothpaste or a gram of cocaine. Everything costs you something inside. The inmates who recognise this the quickest are the ones who tend to survive the longest. Which brings me to Fridays.

To most people on the outside, Fridays represent the end of the working week, which means recreation and downtime over the weekend. It's the opposite for prisoners. Fridays remind them of their family and friends, out there in the world enjoying their freedoms and this can make a lot of inmates very moody. The reality of where they are hits home and so this tends to be when problems often flare up.

A few years back, the prison service recognised all this by introducing what was known as 'Canteen' every Friday. Inmates were permitted to order extra food to be delivered to the prison that day. It was paid for with their own money or cash supplied by their family and friends on the outside. The intention was to help keep inmates more relaxed as the weekend kicked in, as well as giving them something nice to look forward to.

As with so much else inside prison, though, Canteen rapidly evolved into something much more toxic. A lot of the items delivered were soon being used as prison 'currency', which helped fuel a toxic jailhouse black market. This was centred on inmates controlling other prisoners if those debts were not paid in accordance with the so-called 'rules'. Those debts increased in size until the lender decided to call in the loan. Non-payment could result in a severe beating, and the loan still remained intact anyway.

By the time I'd first become a governor, 'Canteen' had already been re-dubbed 'Black Hole Friday' because of the number of fights and clashes between prisoners caused by those items arriving at the jail. A large number of inmates hid in the showers or other prison cubby holes after their shopping was delivered so they could avoid paying back debts from the previous week. And many younger, fitter inmates were forced into becoming debt collectors for older, more experienced prisoners, as it was the only way they could pay off their own debts.

As a result, some inmates imprisoned for non-violent crimes ended up injuring and even killing other prisoners inside jail because they needed to pay off their own mounting debts and had no choice. It had got so bad that staff at the prison where I was governor at that time condemned Canteen as encouraging chaos and many wanted the entire system dismantled. I wasn't able to do that, as I felt like it would breed resentment among many inmates.

However, as governor, I introduced a new rule that all inmates were locked in their cells during deliveries of 'canteen' food. The food packages would be left outside each cell by staff. I hoped this would water down these types of problems. For a few weeks it seemed to work as a state of calmness returned to the prison on Canteen day and staff reported far fewer incidents than in previous weeks. But behind the scenes, debts continued to mount between prisoners that would lead to new, chilling outbreaks of violence.

A few Fridays after the rule had been imposed, one wing PO informed me that a manipulative inmate on the wing had used a Canteen debt to try and force a man to agree to rape a woman prison officer whom the other inmate had fallen out with. The bullied inmate was told he'd be killed unless he either carried out the attack or paid back the debt. When he hesitated, the debt collector said he knew where that prisoner's family lived and would organise a gang to break into their house and rape his teenage daughter. This was a classic Canteen debt spiralling out of control.

The terrified inmate believed he had no choice but to go through with the rape of that female officer. He was told to plan it out and then make sure the debt collector signed off on the details before it could happen. Staff only stumbled on this plan when another inmate overheard the two men discussing the rape. The inmate was so appalled he went to a senior wing PO and reported it.

I confronted the prisoner who was being blackmailed with two senior POs. He confessed but begged us not to make it public knowledge that he'd talked to us because he feared for the safety of his family. So we concocted a story about how the female officer who'd been targeted had to transfer to another prison at short notice because of a staff shortage at that jail.

When we suggested that we also transfer the inmate being blackmailed, he pleaded with us not to because his family would not be able to afford to make the longer journey to see him regularly. I was worried that the debt collector blackmailing the prisoner would attack him in any case, given his victim hadn't carried out his orders. That's when the prison's very own secret justice system kicked in.

A few days later, the blackmailing inmate was seriously injured during an attack in the yard. We never found out who was behind it. That inmate never tried to bully anyone ever again.

Sometimes when running a prison you have no choice but to reluctantly step aside and let the law of the jungle take over.

CHAPTER 27
THE BRIEF

During my long career in the prison service, I've seen the UK justice system close up and never cease to be amazed by the way the legal profession operates. There are certain lawyers defending criminals who seem to work in a bizarre 'no man's land' where they're hired to try and prove a person's innocence when they already know they're guilty. Where is the sense in that?

This can often give hope to the guilty that they might avoid prosecution. But when offenders are found guilty and arrive in prison to serve their sentences, a lot of them seem angry and disillusioned about being overcharged by lawyers who assured them they'd be found innocent.

I want to say now that it's entirely wrong to point the finger at all defence lawyers. A lot of them are fine, upstanding citizens who are vital cogs in the machinery of justice. There is a small cluster of lawyers in this country, however, who've become familiar faces in courthouses and prisons across the UK because they're prepared to defend the indefensible. And they're also the ones who have to watch their own backs due to a wealth of not only embittered clients, but also the police who often look on them as being the blood-suckers of the legal profession.

One such lawyer ended up as an inmate in a men's prison that I took over as governor. He'd laundered stolen money on behalf of one of his richest gangster clients, whom he'd twice managed to get off murder charges. His reward had been a huge fee for cleaning that cash, on top of what he'd already been paid for his legal services. It emerged during his trial that this crooked lawyer's gangster client had deliberately lured him into his illicit activities to ensure he was never tempted to reveal any of his client's secrets to the police.

Within just a few days of arriving at my prison, this lawyer told POs on his wing that two inmates connected to one of his former clients had threatened his life. The lawyer asked to be put in the seg unit for his own protection, but under the prison rules then, I had to be convinced beyond reasonable doubt that his life was in danger before I could even consider it.

Two senior wing POs were sure the lawyer hadn't been threatened at all and was simply trying to manipulate the system. They believed he knew that once he was in the seg unit he could apply to be moved to a 'softer' open prison. But the lawyer continued to insist to the wing staff that he was being threatened on a daily basis. I stood firm and assured my staff I wouldn't allow him to push me into granting the request.

Of course, while I wanted to stand by the rules and not be pressured, if anything did happen to this lawyer, then I'd get all the blame for ignoring his intimidation claims, particularly as I knew he had a lot of friends in high places inside the UK justice system. So I ordered the POs on his wing to maintain a close eye on him to ensure he wasn't harmed.

About four or five days after I'd refused his latest request for a transfer from the wing to the seg unit, the lawyer was beaten up by two inmates in the yard. His attackers were connected to a professional criminal he'd once represented in court – he'd failed to get the criminal off an attempted murder charge.

The wing staff presumed it was a cut-and-dried case of a vengeful prisoner getting his own back on his former lawyer, who'd so spectacularly failed to prevent him going inside. I immediately granted him his request to be transferred to the seg unit. I knew full well this would soon be followed by a move to an open prison but felt I had little choice.

With the lawyer still recovering from his injuries in the health unit of the prison, one of my senior wing POs requested a meeting. He'd been told by one of his most reliable inmate informants that the attack on the lawyer had been deliberately staged in order to enable him to get to the seg wing and moved on to an open prison.

All this had been a reward to the lawyer from another client for not informing police about the murder of a rival drug baron, which this criminal had never been arrested for. I visited the lawyer in the prison health unit and asked him to respond to the allegation. The smarmy look on his face when I questioned him told me everything. Then he arrogantly informed me he'd decided against suing me for exposing him to that wing beating in the first place. I didn't even acknowledge that with a response.

I had wanted to insist he went back on the wing after treatment for his injuries. But instead, I rubber-stamped his move to the seg wing and on to an open prison, despite being convinced the attack was a put-up job.

I'd made a pragmatic decision because I knew it would be impossible to prove the lawyer had set it all up himself. The PO who'd told me the attack was faked never spoke to me again and requested a transfer to another prison. He said to his colleagues he was bitterly disappointed that I'd allowed that lawyer to get away with manipulating the prison system.

In truth I'd found myself stuck between a rock and a hard place. In the prison service, nothing is as simple as you think.

CHAPTER 28
THE HOSTAGE SITUATION

While the majority of inmates keep their heads down and get on with serving their sentences, there are about 10 per cent of them who deliberately cause mayhem. These characters thrive on disrupting prison routine and breaking the rules. That includes bullying and threatening staff, as well as other inmates. But the ultimate act of defiance by a prisoner is to take a hostage. As a PO, I'd already been involved in several such dangerous incidents.

At least now, though, as a governor, I knew it was essential for my staff to be constantly on alert for potential hostage situations because pre-empting them might well end up saving lives. When I started as governor at a prison that housed a notorious 'hostage taker' inmate, whom I'd already encountered when I was a PO, I knew to be wary.

Only a few days after I'd begun this new job, the inmate barricaded up the door to his cell on the seg unit and refused to let anyone enter. He then announced to POs through his door that he'd taken *himself* hostage. He insisted that unless the prison authorities helped him get proper treatment for his mental health problems then he was going to 'kick the shit' out of as many POs as he could lay his hands on.

I knew he'd been in a number of prisons where administrators believed he was faking his mental health problems. He'd always insisted he was the only person who actually realised he needed help, but I believed he should get some form of medical attention. Right now, though, I needed to take charge of the incident in play and work out a way to end it all peacefully. I was well aware that this inmate's behaviour at each prison he'd been to had been getting progressively worse.

Once we had all the other inmates on the seg unit locked down in their cells, a PO who was a specially trained negotiator was dispatched to talk to the prisoner through his locked cell door. Just around the corner from the main corridor, a tactical response unit of POs was on standby, ready to go in to his cell as soon as I gave the word.

The negotiator managed a reasonably friendly conversation with the inmate through the cell door flap, so we remained hopeful we could end the siege quickly and peacefully. Then suddenly the inmate completely stopped talking, stepped away from the door flap he'd been speaking through, turned his back on the negotiator and headed to the far corner of his cell. The negotiator gave me a thumbs down and moved away from the door. I signalled for the staff and tactical response unit to be prepared to move in, but to remain as quiet as possible because I knew any distracting sounds might unnerve him.

For the following two or three minutes, it remained so quiet you could have heard a proverbial pin drop. I could even hear the sound of inmates breathing in the nearby cells. This reminded me that all the prisoners were either right behind their own cell doors or with their ears cupped to the paper-thin walls, listening avidly to everything. Then suddenly, out of nowhere, the entire wing burst into applause and it didn't stop. I couldn't work out why they were doing it at first.

I knew that hostage situations inside prisons made good entertainment for a lot of inmates, especially if POs were at risk of being injured. But this applause caught us all off guard, which very much felt like a bad position to be in. Also, I feared that the noise of it would agitate the prisoner holding himself hostage. However, this didn't quite feel like that. It was as if all the inmates were trying to let this one prisoner know that they realised what he was going through.

As the applause continued, I ordered the negotiator to look through the flap again to see what the inmate himself was doing. She gave me the thumbs up, indicating that he was okay. So, I beckoned the negotiator back to where I was standing alongside the tactical response unit and ordered them all to hold back. Then I walked calmly to each of the doors of the 20 nearest cells on the wing as the applause continued echoing across the wing.

At every one, I quietly explained to the inmates through their cell door why it was essential they stopped clapping for a few minutes while I tried to coax that prisoner out. I promised each of them I'd get him out safe and unharmed, as long as they helped me. I'd put the responsibility back on them.

Most of the inmates immediately complied because they clearly liked and respected this inmate. It might be flattering myself to say, but they also seemed to appreciate the personal nature of my approach to them. Unfortunately, there were a couple of defiant prisoners who ignored me and continued clapping.

As I walked back towards his cell, other inmates began shouting at the clapping prisoners to stop. I was worried that this aggression would make things worse rather than better. But it worked. The entire wing fell completely silent.

I ordered the negotiator and tactical response unit to continue to hold back and moved towards the hostage inmate's cell door. When I opened the flap, he was standing facing the wall at the other end of the cell. I told him what the negotiator had already earlier said; that I'd make sure he got mental health treatment if he ended the siege immediately. At first, he didn't answer, so I repeated what I'd just said.

The corridor was now bathed in complete silence. Every word I said echoed eerily around the entire wing. He turned around and faced me from the other end of his cell. He said he wanted to put a shiv to his own throat and end his life. I knew he was more than capable of doing it. I also realised from my own training that anything I said to him might be used by him as an excuse to kill himself. So I didn't say a word more.

Suddenly, a handful of nearby inmates began yelling through their own locked cell doors at the inmate to give himself up. I was about to ask them to stop when he said he wanted me to unlock the cell door. I hesitated for a split second then gesticulated to the squad and negotiator to stay where they were while I urged three regular POs on standby to join me.

Moments later, I instructed him to start backing out of his cell with his hands in the air while we unlocked the door. As he backed into the corridor, the three POs cuffed him. All the POs standing by broke into spontaneous applause, followed by all the inmates from their cells.

It was an overwhelmingly emotional moment. We'd all joined forces to avoid a tragedy. Sometimes, in prison, stories can end happily.

CHAPTER 29
BROKEN

When POs and inmates have genuine respect for one another, prisons can be surprisingly calm places. I was serving as governor at one men's prison when I came across a senior wing PO who took the care and welfare of inmates to another level. He told me that he hated the way the prison system flattened the emotions of inmates. He said he hoped that I, the new governor, would dismantle the archaic, old-fashioned rules that he and some staff believed added to the tension inside the prison.

In many ways, this senior wing PO reminded me of myself almost 20 years earlier. He was full of radical ideas but little notion of how to actually instigate those changes. His most revolutionary idea was a prison job system that rewarded inmates for their productivity. It sounded good in theory, but some of his fellow colleagues thought he was 'weak' for showing any interest in such issues. Some also complained to me that this PO was guilty of favouritism towards some specific inmates on his wing and that this was upsetting a lot of the other prisoners. It was clear that these complaints were mainly motivated by officers who disapproved of this PO's methods, so I tended to ignore them.

Rather confusingly, a few days later, this same suppos-edly 'soft' wing PO had a stand-up argument in a corridor with one of the inmates he'd earlier been accused of favour-ing. Two other officers had to drag him off the prisoner to avoid a full-on fight. No one was seriously hurt so I chose not to bring disciplinary charges against either the PO or the inmate. I considered it a one-off incident and nothing more.

But shortly after this, a senior wing PO filed a report to me stating that the officer in question had been behav-ing 'very strangely' since the day before that incident. He'd only just avoided a scuffle with another prisoner. Then this senior officer found the PO close to tears in the staff locker room after finishing a shift. When he asked the PO what was wrong, the officer told him to mind his own fucking business, smashed the door to his locker shut and walked out.

I was as puzzled as the officer who'd reported all this to me. But since it was the end of the week, I decided to think about what to do over the weekend and then take appropriate action when we were all back on duty on Monday.

Within minutes of getting to my office that Monday morning, a large number of staff turned up and explained that the same PO had lost his temper in the staff locker room for a second time that morning when a colleague ribbed him about the fight he'd had the previous week with the inmate. They had to be pulled apart in the end.

The other officer involved insisted he didn't want to press charges against his colleague because he believed the wing PO must have some personal issues, which were impacting on his behaviour. None of the POs seemed able to actually explain what those issues were, though, so we were all a little in the dark.

Just 10 minutes later, this once innovative officer came to see me to say he was resigning from the prison service because he realised he was no longer mentally fit to serve effectively inside a prison. I asked him what had caused such a sudden change in his personality. He insisted it was nothing important, but it was obvious he was hiding something.

It's hard to help someone if they won't actually tell you what has happened to them. All sorts of things went through my head. Had he had a romantic relationship with an inmate? Or had he taken a bribe from one of the inmates he'd earlier favoured? In prison, I'd learned to rule nothing out.

In the space of just a few weeks since I'd taken over as governor, he'd gone from being the PO I admired more than anyone else on the staff to being a dangerous troublemaker seemingly on the verge of violence all the time. So I pressed him. Why was he throwing away a good career?

He looked broken when I asked him. I could tell I was close and repeated the question. He looked at me awkwardly and paused. Then, following a sharp intake of breath, he told me how he'd recently found out that his 12-year-old son had been abused by a teacher at his school. He said that he'd arrived at work the day after finding out what had happened filled with anger and hatred.

His opinion of prisons had completely changed. He no longer looked on inmates as vulnerable people who needed his help. They'd suddenly all become his enemy. So when one inmate cracked a joke about underage sex, he'd lost it. He knew he shouldn't have but he couldn't hold back because there was so much anger inside him.

He said it was also guilt. He felt he was to blame for what had happened to his child, as he worked such long hours that his son had been out when he shouldn't have been. After that, he'd found he couldn't even bear to look an inmate in the eye in case that prisoner had ever done something as horrible as what had been done to his son.

He also felt as if what had happened to his son was some sort of punishment for him because he'd previously been so accepting towards the inmates. All his hopes and aspirations as a prison officer had been dissolved by the assault on his son. However, he had the humility to realise that if he'd continued working as a prison officer, he was going to lose it over and over again and seriously injure or maybe even kill an inmate or colleague, which was why he was stepping away.

Many weeks later, I asked a prison psychiatrist I knew whether I should have tried to get that PO some professional help and then encouraged him to return to work. He summed the situation up perfectly by saying: "It's not just what happens to you or your loved ones that causes the damage. It's how *you* deal with it."

The preventative measures that officer took himself were admirable. But I keep wondering how many other fucked-up prison staff there are across the service who are close to breaking point.

CHAPTER 30
THE MADAM

I've often found that the more unusual the prisoner, the more challenging they can turn out to be. At one prison where I was governor, I encountered one of the most perceptive inmates I'd ever met. In many ways, she was like someone out of an old-fashioned spy novel. She'd been imprisoned for living off what is known in UK law as 'immoral earnings' after running a brothel in the centre of London. In other words, she was a madam.

Inside prison, she'd been dubbed 'the agony aunt' on her wing because she'd become the go-to person when it came to listening to the problems of other inmates and then handing out common-sense advice. I was surprised at first that a woman from such a hard-nosed background could be so patient and understanding.

She even insisted she'd never forced any of the women who worked for her to sell their bodies and claimed she only ever recruited women 'who were looking for a bit of an adventure'. She also proudly boasted that some of the women who'd worked for her had ended up marrying their clients and cited this as further proof that her business was respectable. But when it comes to people's sexual habits, there are always deep and dark secrets lurking beneath the surface.

At the beginning of her much-publicised trial, the madam's lawyer referred to numerous politicians, aristo-crats and even members of the royal family being among her regular clients. It was alleged in court that she'd kept a black book containing all the details of those rich and famous people. And during the opening of her trial, there was huge media speculation that she was going to name some of these clients while giving evidence in her defence.

Then halfway through the hearing, she changed her plea to guilty after agreeing a deal with prosecutors for a relatively short sentence. She ended up getting two years and the contents of the alleged black book were never publicly disclosed.

Back in my prison, this elderly woman – she was, by this time, in her mid-sixties – was a model inmate, appreciated by staff and inmates alike. While she seemed respectable in many senses, I'd learned down the years in the prison busi-ness that people's moods can change with the flick of a switch.

Senior officers on the madam's wing reported that after months of giving out free advice to those who asked, she'd started refusing to talk to anyone. And then she'd begun trying to pick fights with other inmates, and most nights, she could be heard crying into her pillow.

The staff had no doubt she was showing clear signs of depression, not least of which was a passionate self-loathing. They requested that she should be kept under a discreet suicide watch. My staff also reported that the madam's complete change of character had seemed to coincide with a visit from her lawyer to the prison a few days earlier. She'd refused, however, to talk to anyone about what had upset her, so it was hard to know what had happened. I tried to arrange a meeting with her but she claimed to POs that she had the flu and didn't want to give it to me. I didn't force the issue as I had no wish to put her under any more pressure.

A couple of days later, a UK prison service administrator contacted me to say that the police had requested that the madam was moved to the seg unit immediately 'for her own safety'. No other reason was given, but it was made clear I had little choice in the matter, so I ordered the transfer. I wondered why the police were still taking an interest in the madam's case so many months after her court case had finished.

Three days after she was transferred to the seg unit, two police detectives visited her in prison and then, later that same day, she tried to hang herself with a towel wrapped around the bars of her cell window. She was only saved because staff were keeping a close eye on her after becoming worried about her rapidly deteriorating mental health.

While the madam recovered from her suicide attempt in the prison's health wing, I contacted the police to ask them why she'd been so upset by their meeting. They told me it was a 'confidential matter' and insisted that what they'd discussed with her was 'of no concern' to me.

I was so incensed by their attitude that I discreetly launched my own enquiries by talking to the staff who knew her best. One senior PO revealed to me that she'd told him that she'd refused to hand over that black book with all the names of her most famous clients to the police. The madam also said to the PO that the police had warned her that her decision would put her in danger. After hearing this, I ordered staff to keep her under a 24-hour watch in the prison's health wing where she was still recovering from her suicide attempt.

That afternoon, a PO on duty at the health unit found the madam standing by an open window. He was convinced she'd been about to jump out of it and would have done so if he hadn't arrived and coaxed her away. The following morning I visited her bedside.

For at least 15 minutes she refused to even acknowledge my presence. It was very frustrating. I assured her that we wanted to protect her and tried to subtly let her know that I was aware of the background to the earlier police visit and how much it must have upset her. She still refused to say a word, so I got up to leave.

"I wasn't really going to kill myself," she suddenly whispered. "I just wanted to get out of the seg unit because they could have got me in there."

I asked her whom she was scared of and she talked about the black book containing all those VIPs' names. She said she'd kept it as 'insurance'. She claimed the police and her lawyer had warned her she would be charged with new offences – which could mean another five years in prison – unless she handed that black book over to Scotland Yard.

She believed they planned to destroy the book to protect all the famous names who'd used the brothel she ran. Either way, she'd arranged for the black book to be delivered to a newspaper office in the event of her sudden death.

I asked her why up to now she'd been protecting those rich and famous clientele. After all, they didn't care about her. She looked very uncomfortable when I asked the question and admitted she'd fallen in love with one of those names in the black book and didn't want to hurt him or destroy his marriage. She refused to say who he was, except that she knew he would never leave his wife for her. I couldn't go to the police because if she was telling the truth, then they were part of the same conspiracy to protect her rich and powerful clients.

Less than a week later, the madam's sentence was suddenly commuted by the Home Office, who announced she'd been given 'special dispensation' because of unforeseen circumstances. There was no proper explanation as to why she was being released. I was ordered by UK Justice to arrange for her to be secretly escorted out of the prison in the middle of the night to avoid anyone knowing she'd even left.

The following day, I called her lawyer and asked him why she'd been released so suddenly. Initially, he refused to discuss it. But after I pressed him, he said she'd agreed to hand over the black book in exchange for an immediate release from prison, plus a generous monthly cash allowance and free residency in a picturesque cottage on the edge of a lake owned by a British aristocrat.

If you can't beat the system then I guess the next best thing is to join it. But that wily old madam's skilful exit strategy meant the UK's rich and powerful remain as protected as ever.

CHAPTER 31
MISCONCEPTION

Most inmates keep such a low profile that they're usually overlooked when anything is written about prison life. But often it's the quiet ones who turn out to have committed the most surprising offences.

I came across this some years into my career as a governor when I was running what I can only describe as a very laid-back women's prison. It made a refreshing change from most of the institutions that I'd run previously. The inmates seemed almost as content as the ones I'd met when I'd earlier been training to be a governor in that special prison within a prison, where only one PO was left in charge of all the offenders.

A lot of the relaxed atmosphere this time was almost certainly down to my predecessor as governor, who'd thrown out many of the petty rules after taking over. I wanted to continue this tradition and made a point of assuring every inmate in that prison personally this would be the case, within days of taking over.

Among them was a group of about a dozen older inmates who looked and behaved more like residents in an old folk's home than hardened prisoners. The first time I met them in the common area, two of them were actually knitting jumpers for their grandchildren. Knitting needles were classified as potential weapons inside most prisons, but none of the staff seemed bothered by them in this jail. When I asked a senior wing PO why, she pointed out that there hadn't been a violent offence in this prison for more than two years. In any case, she said, all the knitting needles were always handed in at the end of each day.

Among those elderly inmates was one woman who wore round, wire-rimmed glasses, a short grey bob hairstyle and a very drab blue cardigan with tracksuit bottoms and beige, chunky orthopaedic-type shoes like something a nurse would have worn in the 1950s. She'd continued maniacally knitting away throughout my visit, without once looking up. I deliberately didn't ask the PO accompanying me what she was inside for because I always tried to avoid doing that in front of staff and inmates.

On returning to my office later that morning, I looked up her file as I was curious about her. I'd presumed she was inside for some kind of fraud or maybe just shoplifting. In fact, she was a trained chemist who'd worked for a millionaire drug baron and had helped flood the northern half of the UK with crystal methamphetamine.

During her court case, police testified that tens of thousands of people had been turned into meth addicts by the drugs she'd helped manufacture. Her defence counsel had claimed that she'd only joined the gang because her teenage grandson had a rare form of cancer and she needed to pay for specialist treatment for him in the US.

It was revealed in court that the drug baron's own son had had a similar life-threatening condition and that the pair had first met at the hospital where the children were being treated. The court also heard that the drug lord offered the chemist a big cash advance to help with her grandson's medical bills in the US on condition she worked for him. After that, it didn't take her long to master the art of manufacturing crystal meth, thanks to her training as a chemist.

Tragically, her grandchild died six months later during what was supposed to be his life-saving surgery in the US. However, even after this, the drug baron wouldn't allow her to leave the gang because she was so good at making crystal meth. Her lawyer alleged in court that the narco had threatened to kill her other family members if she tried to quit.

She ended up manufacturing more than £20 million worth of crystal meth over a five-year period, according to one police witness. The chemist's mitigating circumstances seemed very relevant to me, but they had little influence on the judge, who gave her a 12-year prison sentence.

Back in my prison, she was said by staff to be one of the quietest inmates they'd ever encountered. She'd even steadfastly refused any advice from prison welfare services on how to cope with being in jail. Even more surprisingly, she hadn't had one visitor in all the time she'd been in my prison.

I asked one senior officer on the chemist's wing if she appeared depressed. But he insisted she was fine. He said she was an avid reader and seemed very content in her own little world away from most of the other inmates, apart from that small group of elderly prisoners.

When I first saw her, I thought I'd noticed a void of emptiness in her eyes. Now I realised why. Losing her grandchild had probably marked the beginning of the end of her life.

* * *

Life in that particular prison turned out to be extremely uneventful. The only moment of significance was when half a dozen inmates suffered food poisoning. It had been severe enough for them all to have to be treated in the prison's health unit. But they all quickly recovered.

Then about a fortnight later, a middle-aged female PO collapsed when she was getting in her car to drive home from work late one afternoon. Two other officers found her unconscious on the car park tarmac. She was immediately taken by ambulance to hospital. Most staff presumed she'd had a heart attack or stroke.

At the hospital, though, tests indicated that the PO might have suffered some form of food poisoning. It was clearly much more serious than those previous incidents because she was extremely ill. Medical staff admitted they couldn't effectively treat her until they'd ascertained the exact cause of the food poisoning in the first place. Two of the PO's closest staff colleagues rang me in tears from the hospital to say that doctors had said her life was hanging by a thread and her husband and children were at her bedside.

As the news filtered through the prison that morning, I received a deputation of POs from the wing where the officer had worked. They were convinced the chemist was involved in her collapse but none of them seemed prepared to explain the reasons behind their accusations. They said that the chemist had refused to leave her cell since she'd heard the news and was in tears most of the time. When I visited the wing to try and persuade the chemist to talk to me, she refused to utter a word.

As I left the wing, one of the oldest inmates – who was part of the knitting group – got in a row with one of the women POs right in front of me. When I stepped between them, the inmate asked to speak to me in private away from my staff. In the wing PO's office, she told me the chemist and the hospitalised officer had had a sexual relationship, which had ended badly when the same PO refused to leave her husband for her.

Later that day, I summoned the two senior POs on her wing to my office. They admitted they knew about the relationship but hadn't mentioned it earlier out of consideration for the PO's husband and children. They said they were convinced the chemist had concocted some kind of poison and then tested it out earlier on those prisoners, who'd also got sick.

They believed that after they recovered, the chemist decided to make her poison stronger in order to kill her estranged lover. The two officers also said they had evidence that the chemist had put the poison in a hot drink, which she'd then given to the PO.

They produced a clip from a prison CCTV camera which showed the chemist handing her lover a hot drink in the wing kitchen not long before she collapsed in the car park. It wasn't conclusive evidence by any means, so I decided to confront the chemist herself.

Later that afternoon, two officers escorted her into my office. She looked as white as a sheet and was shivering from head to toe. I asked her if she was all right. She said she was still in shock about the hospitalised PO. Then she tearfully opened up about their relationship. She confirmed she'd made her a hot drink on the day she'd collapsed, but she insisted she hadn't poisoned anyone, least of all 'the love of my life', as she described the PO.

While the chemist was still in my office, I got a call. It was the police saying that the officer in hospital had died and that they were planning to launch a murder investigation once the post mortem was completed. Unfortunately, the chemist heard enough of that phone call to know what had happened. She fainted on the spot and had to be revived by the two POs, who then escorted her back to her cell.

Down on the wing, unbeknown to me, prison staff began secretly feeding inmates information about the chemist because they were so angry about what had happened to their colleague. Two of the inmates who'd been originally poisoned tried to attack the chemist and had to be pulled off her by three officers, so I had to immediately transfer her to the seg unit. Everyone was pointing the finger of suspicion at the chemist, but she still insisted she'd done nothing wrong beyond having a relationship with the victim.

The pathologist examining the PO's remains eventually confirmed that toxicology tests showed that the PO had suffered the same type of food poisoning as the earlier victims. However, the officer had a previously undetected congenital heart defect, which meant the poison had brought on a heart attack, and that was what had killed her, not the actual food poisoning. The pathologist stated that this type of food poisoning was extremely common and the majority of victims usually recovered easily, as had been the case with the other victims. He also said that such food poisoning could not be deliberately administered, so the police immediately dropped their murder investigation.

Back inside the prison, though, the chemist was still public enemy number one. People remained convinced she had something to do with it. She remained in isolation in the seg unit, rarely speaking to any staff or inmates and still receiving no visitors. In the end, I had no choice but to transfer her to a special seg unit in a prison in another part of the UK for her own safety.

She was eventually released from prison early for good behaviour. I heard she changed her identity and went to live abroad. Yes, she'd broken the law but I don't believe she was a real criminal in the widely accepted sense of the word. All she'd really wanted to do was save the life of her sickly grandson.

In the end, though, it cost her everything.

CHAPTER 32
THE BUTCHER

It's believed that a third of all prisoners have got away with more crimes than the ones that landed them in jail in the first place. And the secrets those inmates hide are undoubtedly responsible for much of the paranoia and violence inside prisons.

Sometimes those unprosecuted offences are so serious that the prisoner in question turns out to be a lot more dangerous than we were originally led to believe. This then constitutes a threat to the security of a prison's staff and its inmates. Also, if a prisoner is released back into society having not been punished for their *other* hidden crimes, especially violent ones, there is also the safety of the general public to consider.

All these issues came to a head for me as a governor when the police made an unprecedented request for help from me and my staff to try and bring a criminal to justice. The criminal in question was an inmate in my prison who'd been found guilty of cutting up and disposing of murder victims for a crime family. He'd even been nicknamed The Butcher in the tabloids.

Detectives were convinced The Butcher had killed at least half a dozen women in the north-east of England who had no direct connection to the crime gang. He was, they said, a secret serial killer. The details of the killings were shocking. According to the police, he'd lured his victims into cars late at night by pretending to be a taxi driver. Then he'd rape, kill and dismember them, often in woodland near where they came from.

Police had uncovered a shallow grave in a wood that contained two of the serial killer's victims' torsos without arms, legs and heads. A forensic examiner had concluded that the way the liver and kidneys had been removed from both torsos suggested the killer most likely planned to cook them.

The police had learned from one underworld source inside that their prime suspect often used to turn up at his crime gang's headquarters with fresh cuts of 'meat' for his bosses, who were unaware it came from human beings. Detectives also believed that the suspect had been incredibly careful to ensure no one in that gang ever suspected he was an actual serial killer.

The police only had circumstantial evidence to prove his link to the murders. They needed either a full confession from him or at least some very substantial evidence in order to prosecute. They wanted us to convince another inmate who had worked alongside their alleged serial killer in the same gang to help bring their suspect to justice. Police believed this inmate would know enough about their suspect's movements at the time of some of the killings to help nail their man.

When the police first approached me, it sounded like a desperately naive plan. How on earth could my staff and I persuade a hardened inmate to break the oldest code of the underworld: *Thou shalt not inform on another criminal*?

There was also an ominous ticking clock aspect to all this because The Butcher was due for release from prison just three months later for those lesser gangland offences. Once out, he'd most likely start killing young women again, according to detectives.

All my senior POs who attended a meeting with the police predicted that this inmate's criminal associate on the wing would immediately dismiss the serial killer accusations as being made up by the police. And he'd most likely then tell the suspect exactly what was happening. But they all agreed to keep a close watch on the suspect and his gang associate in the hope of finding an opening, which the police could exploit in order to bring the serial killer to justice.

To their credit, two wing POs quickly discovered that The Butcher had fallen out with his crime gang associate on the wing over a prison debt. The police insisted on immediately interviewing the associate, although they decided not to yet mention that they suspected his fellow gang member of being a serial killer. They wanted to sound him out first.

Within minutes of starting their interview, though, the police hit a brick wall. The inmate assumed the detectives suspected him of being involved in another killing that both men had witnessed when they worked for the same crime gang, and then refused to answer any questions until his lawyer was present. He also pointed out that his gang bosses would come after him if they thought he was helping the police in any way.

I thought the police had been way too heavy-handed. They'd put this inmate under too much pressure and it had blown up badly in their faces. I also had no doubt he'd inform the serial killer that the police were investigating that murder to avoid any accusation that he'd been helping them.

The police insisted he wouldn't do that because he'd fallen out with their suspect, but the two men lived in cells only 20 yards apart on the same wing and, feud or no feud, I was sure they'd share that kind of information, particularly as it was in the informant's interests.

Meanwhile, the lawyer informed police that his client would not be cooperating with detectives and so the entire serial killer investigation collapsed before it had even got properly going. And, even less surprisingly, The Butcher soon heard that his fellow gang member inmate had been 'helping the police with their enquiries'. He presumed, as the other inmate had, that detectives were trying to nail them both for their involvement in that other gang murder.

With the entire police operation suspended, I was left to pick up the pieces. I had to ensure there were no recriminations connected to the alleged serial killer, who luckily still had no idea the police were looking at him for multiple murders.

Back on the wing, the friction between these two inmates began to worsen, as each was deeply suspicious of the other. Eventually, one of the senior wing POs recommended that one of them was either sent to another prison or at least put in the seg wing to separate them. But the police still had hopes of solving the case and insisted that the pair shouldn't be split up and that there was still the possibility of getting their informant to help.

It was clear, though, that the police had little concern for the safety of the inmate who'd already refused to help them. It felt to me as if they'd completely lost perspective when it came to the risks they were running, and, as governor, I was obliged to protect that inmate, as well as everyone else on the wing. My staff informed me that other prisoners on the wing had already started presuming the police's uncooperative informant was a gangland 'grass'.

Detectives then announced to me that they'd decided to take a different approach to their investigation. They were going to interview the criminal associate of the serial killer suspect a second time with his lawyer present. And this time they'd tell him about the serial killing allegations against his fellow gang member.

I was present at that meeting as the inmate was shown pictures of the bodies of the victims and some of the evidence that linked the suspect to the murders. I remember thinking at that time it was strange that he didn't seem at all shocked.

The gangster inmate ended up looking at each of the most gruesome photos at least three times as he sat in silence in the interview room. He was then informed by detectives there were only a couple of weeks until this alleged serial killer was going to be released from prison. They asked him if he could

live with himself if the suspect went back to killing more innocent women.

The gangster inmate put the last of the photos down on the
table in front of him and told the detectives he still wouldn't
help them. He then asked his lawyer to tell them he wanted
to be taken back to his cell. The infuriated police immediately
concluded that their suspect must have already threatened to
kill this inmate and that this had to be why he'd refused to help.

But I wasn't so sure. He just hadn't seemed surprised
enough to hear about the serial killer allegations. Within
48 hours, my wing staff were reporting that the serial killer
suspect was actually the one who seemed to think he was
under threat. He was refusing to come out of his cell and one
PO said he and other staff believed that the suspected serial
killer had been intimidated by someone else, who'd been
shadowing him around the wing most of the time.

I went back to the police to demand that their suspect was
either moved to the seg unit or another prison. It took them
two days to return my calls but we finally agreed he should be
transferred later that day to another jail.

That afternoon, the suspected serial killer was found
dead in the showers an hour before he was due to be transferred. He'd been stabbed at least 20 times and the coroner
said afterwards that it looked like a frenzied attack carried out
by at least five different people, who'd all taken it in turns to
puncture his body.

The murder was immediately rumoured in the prison to
have been carried out because the victim was a gang member

suspected of being a police informant. The fact he was a suspected serial killer still wasn't known to the general prison population, it seemed.

The inmates who committed the murder were never unmasked, despite an extensive prison investigation by the service and murder squad detectives. The police even ordered a forensic expert to examine the inmate who'd refused to help their serial killer investigation. They found no evidence linking him to the murder and he also had a good alibi.

One of the detectives later told me that one of their sources told them that their serial killer suspect had actually been killed because his one-time gangster bosses feared that if he was arrested for those serial killings, he'd probably inform on the rest of the gang in the hope of getting a lighter sentence.

You may have different feelings having read this story, about whether it was better to have this happen rather than risk him being the one who committed more killings. But above all else, it remained my primary duty as governor to ensure that inmates and staff were kept safe and that they did not think they were above the law.

CHAPTER 33
IMPOSTERS

Older professional criminals are always on the lookout for ways to manipulate the prison system, and some POs even play along with these inclinations by accepting 'gifts' from such criminals. This could be anything from a new mobile phone to a top-of-the-range TV set for doing them 'a favour'.

I first learned about this culture of corruption when I was a young PO and a senior officer on my wing urged me to take whatever gift was offered by one particularly rich mobster inmate. This officer reckoned it would help keep the peace, although I had little doubt it was just down to good old-fashioned greed. When I pointed out that this broke the prison rules, the officer told me to mind my own fucking business and then carried on with his own corrupt activities.

A couple of years later, he was caught red-handed by police handling a shipment of drugs on behalf of the same man who'd bribed him in prison, no doubt the price he had to pay for accepting those favours. There are quite a number of these 'bad egg' POs operating in plain sight throughout the service and a lot of them don't even think they've done anything wrong.

I call them 'imposters'. The cleverest ones often wear a lot of camouflage, including happy-go-lucky smiles and excellent manners. Beneath that smooth veneer, I always believed they were hiding a myriad of dark intentions, which unfortunately being a prison officer seems to sometimes help fuel.

By around 2008, UK prison officers were being fired at the rate of three a week for offences including fraud, corruption and even sleeping with inmates. And ever since I'd become a governor, I'd been determined to smoke them out. It annoyed me that I hadn't been proactive enough about them when I was a PO during my early days in the service, but you could argue I never quite had enough power to do so anyway.

The key to bringing these imposters to justice is to always make sure there is enough evidence to nail them when you confront them. I knew from experience that some were even capable of framing honest prison staff to get themselves off the hook, so you need to have everything to bury them there and then.

The vast majority of crooked POs begin their treachery with something as simple as supplying an inmate with tobacco in exchange for some money. But, whether they know it or not, this often leads to drug smuggling. And once an officer has allowed himself to be manipulated into doing something illegal for an inmate, it's a long road back to honesty.

The majority of corrupt POs I've come across cite money as their primary motivation for breaking the law inside prison. I would say from experience, this issue is a lot more complex than being purely just about greed. Inmates know that once they've got an officer 'onside' they can play them any way they want. Some prisoners go out of their way to protect their favourite crooked POs, knowing full well this gives them even more leverage inside jail.

I'd been about to expose one crooked PO at a prison I ran when he was killed in a car crash. He was actually on his way to meet a criminal who'd had him on his payroll ever since first meeting in prison. This gangster even had the gall to send a wreath to the PO's funeral.

When I'd earlier been a PO, I'd served at one prison where an officer known as Mr B struck so much fear into his own colleagues that many wing staff were too terrified to ever accuse him of being crooked, even though he clearly was. Some of the PO's friends even tried to convince me that all the allegations against him had been made up by inmates, who hated him because he was so honest. I simply didn't buy that.

I heard rumours that Mr B had one fellow officer beaten up by a prisoner when that PO threatened to report Mr B to the governor for accepting a bribe. This allegation was never fully substantiated at the time, but it seemed to have a ring of truth to it. Then one lunchtime I was on canteen duty when I saw an ex-bank robber turned drug baron pass Mr B what appeared to be an envelope. I'll never forget the look on Mr B's face when he glanced up and saw me watching him.

Shortly after that, I was told I was being posted to another prison, despite having served less than three months on the wing. When I asked the assistant governor why I was being transferred, he said there were staff shortages at the other prison. I later found out that wasn't really the reason. Another PO told me that Mr B had complained that I wasn't experienced enough to work in such a big prison.

The day before I was due to depart that jail, I walked into an open cell during rec time and found Mr B deep in conversation with the same inmate I'd seen him receive that envelope from in the canteen weeks earlier. Both of them looked irritated by my presence that morning, so I timidly apologised and left the cell immediately. True, that apparent transaction didn't actually prove anything in itself, but to this day I still regret that I decided not to report it.

* * *

Nine years on, and as a fully fledged prison governor, I felt I needed to make amends. I'd just been posted back to that same prison as governor on short notice after the previous one had been fired for allowing inmates to do the gardening at his family home. At first, I was astonished to find Mr B was still working there. I'd presumed his illegal activities would have been exposed by this time.

The outgoing governor even left me a note outlining the situation with Mr B and referred to allegations that he'd blackmailed other officers and inmates not to give evidence against him on at least three occasions. This had ensured no corruption charges were ever brought against him.

Determined to finally bring him to justice, I arranged the transfer of two trusted, trouble-shooting POs I knew from another prison to work alongside Mr B. He was told there were shortages on the wing and these two officers were on temporary assignment.

I couldn't inform anyone inside the prison what I was doing in case Mr B got to hear about it. This troubled me greatly because I didn't like breaking the trust of my staff but I was determined that this crooked officer would be taken down at all costs this time.

The two POs I brought in to work on the wing with Mr B spent weeks observing him without coming up with one shred of evidence of corruption whatsoever. They even queried the accuracy of my original allegations against Mr B. They suggested that maybe he was nothing more than a brash character who'd rubbed staff and inmates up the wrong way, which, of course, did not mean he was corrupt.

I don't deny I was out to get Mr B. It felt personal after what had happened when I was a PO. I knew I was going to have to be one step ahead of him if I was going to succeed, though. So I ordered my two spies to continue observing Mr B. To me, corruption was like venom running through the 'vein' of the service and if we continued looking the other way, then it would only get worse.

I didn't want staff working in my prisons to be even suspected of corruption, let alone actually taking bribes. I wasn't like some other governors who often shrugged their shoulders and talked about how POs were so good at their jobs that it didn't matter if they accepted the odd 'gift'. So I sent my two spies back on the wing with their tails between their legs and ordered them to ratchet up their efforts to catch

Mr B in the act. Within a week, they'd heard him boasting on the wing that he'd stayed at a holiday complex in Spain owned by the same gangster I'd seen give him that envelope all those years earlier.

At last, we seemed to have a breakthrough, so I summoned Mr B to my office and confronted him about it. He wasn't at all bothered and openly admitted he'd stayed at the resort, although insisted he'd paid for it all himself after being recommended to the holiday complex by that same former inmate. He knew only too well that none of this proved he was actually guilty of corruption.

Then I made a big mistake. Just before he left my office, instead of letting him think he'd got one over on me which could tempt him to do something corrupt, I mentioned to him what I'd seen him do in the prison canteen nearly 10 years earlier, when he took an envelope from that crime boss.

He nodded slowly while staring straight at me as I recalled the incident. Then – without uttering another word – he jumped up and stormed out of my office. Later that same day, he complained to his union rep that I was trying to intimidate him.

I was infuriated with myself for being such an idiot. I'd laid my cards out on the table in front of him, so now he most likely realised I was waiting for him to put a foot wrong. However, a few days later, my two spies heard rumours on the wing that Mr B had been given a £20,000 watch as a birthday gift by one of the wing's most notorious inmates, a professional gangster.

Before I'd had chance to haul him in for questioning, though, the wing POs reported that Mr B and his gangster 'friend' – who was supposed to have given him that watch – had been involved in a fight with each other in a corridor of the wing. My two spies soon found out from other inmates that the gangster and Mr B had fallen out because the mobster had worked out that Mr B was under surveillance by my two men. As such, he felt that Mr B was attracting too much attention, which was impacting on his criminal activities on the wing.

When I interviewed Mr B the next morning about the alleged watch, I steeled myself for a confrontation, but he was far less defiant than before. He admitted he'd made a few stupid mistakes but insisted he was not a crooked officer and claimed that the watch story had been planted by the gangster inmate because he had a grudge against him. Knowing the background, I sort of believed him. But just in case he was lying, I simply nodded and said nothing, unlike last time.

Then his demeanour changed even further. I noticed his leg twitching and in a hesitant voice he disclosed that his life and that of his family was being threatened and he wanted the prison service to protect him.

When I asked him why, he explained that the previous evening he'd been followed home by two men in a silver BMW. The vehicle had stayed on his tail all the way to his house and he believed it was a message telling him that his family were at risk.

At first, I wondered if this was all another lie. Maybe this was his way of wriggling out of an awkward situation? But his eyes began watering up and he seemed genuinely terrified. I felt I couldn't send him into the firing line, in case he or his family were harmed, even though I was still convinced he was crooked.

I'd always promised myself I would never again brush these types of issues under the carpet but, in the end, I realised the only way to stop the criminals who were after him and his family was for him to step away from his job as a prison officer immediately. I could have taken the case further and no doubt nailed him for corruption. However, there was always the chance he might get off all corruption charges against him, so I simply let him know he'd run out of lives and unless he went for good, I would indeed pursue him all the way to the courts.

At least I'd removed a classic imposter from the prison service for good, without dragging it through the courts at great expense to the taxpayer. Mr B left the prison that morning without saying goodbye to any of his colleagues. It was clear that his criminal friends had deliberately turned him over, so I hadn't exactly brought him to justice. But I believed this was the next best thing.

Hopefully, a lot of toxic old dinosaurs like Mr B have now left the prison service. But you can never be certain.

CHAPTER 34
THE CONFESSION

Surprises come thick and fast inside prisons. One day everything's calm and trouble-free and then suddenly something happens and you get hit straight in the face with a sledgehammer. After a month of peace and tranquillity inside one of the biggest prisons where I served as governor, a long-term inmate called Rocky requested a meeting through a senior wing officer about 'a confidential matter'.

As governor, I was well used to getting these types of requests from prisoners and usually I relied on my staff to advise me whether to see them. Inmates often demanded meetings that ended up being a complete waste of time because their complaints were either petty or just plain, downright lies. But since Rocky had a reputation as one of the brightest and best-behaved inmates on his wing, I decided to see him.

He'd been a very rich and successful financier until he murdered his wife, which had resulted in a 15-year jail sentence. Wife-killers are not the most popular inmates in most prisons for obvious reasons, but staff said Rocky had cleverly turned that around by offering prisoners free financial advice from his cell.

After turning up at my office for the meeting he'd requested, Rocky immediately asked me if the PO who'd escorted him from the wing could not sit in on our conversation. This was awkward for me as I didn't want in any way to imply that this officer was untrustworthy. Fortunately, this PO didn't object and agreed to wait in the reception area outside my office.

Rocky started by saying that what he was about to tell me was 'mind-blowing' and insisted it was 100 per cent true. A lot of inmates try to reel you in this way. Then he informed me, straight-faced, that one of the POs on his wing had confessed to him that he'd murdered his own wife.

I'd heard just about everything when it came to prisoners' allegations against staff but this was a first. And it was even more bizarre because of Rocky's own offence. I asked Rocky why on earth this PO would have made such a confession to him in the first place. Without hesitating, Rocky explained that he'd got on so well with this PO that they'd talked a lot about their families and childhood.

"And that's when I discovered we had something more in common," explained Rocky. "I thought long and hard before coming here to tell you all this, guv. That officer's a decent fellow. But his kids need to know the truth, right?"

None of this was actual evidence that the PO in question had murdered his wife, and I found it hard to judge the truthfulness of Rocky's claims. When I asked him to provide further details of this alleged murder, he admitted he knew nothing more. Assuming it might smoke him out if he was lying, I gave him one last chance to retract what he'd just told me.

"Have you got a grudge against this officer?" I asked Rocky.

He shook his head, looked deeply offended and still insisted it was true.

Rocky's allegations actually left me stranded in a kind of no man's land. I couldn't see why he would lie about it, but he wasn't very convincing, having not been able to provide any further proof. Plus, his own conviction for killing his wife still didn't exactly inspire me to believe anything he'd said.

Under prison rules, though, I was obliged to look into any such claims from an inmate about a PO. I told Rocky I'd make some discreet enquiries before deciding whether to let the authorities know. He looked disappointed when I said that.

"Why would I lie to you about this, guv?" he said, before getting up to leave. "It's painful to bring all this up because it's a reminder of what I did. I wish he hadn't said it, but he did."

After he'd left, I logged into the officer's file on my desktop computer to check out his background. His notes referred to a couple of disciplinary issues that occurred during a difficult break-up from his wife five years earlier. She'd apparently walked out on him and their children. The notes stated that he'd eventually settled down after the marriage was annulled. Surprisingly, he'd been awarded sole custody of the couple's children, then aged four and seven.

Then I noticed a small reference in the report to how the police had briefly been involved with the case after some of the wife's relatives complained that none of them had heard from her since she'd walked out on her husband. But the police quickly dropped their enquiries because they'd been unable to find any evidence of foul play.

If this PO turned out to be completely innocent, then it would be extremely damaging to him and his family if these allegations ever got out. And if he was guilty, then it was important he didn't get wind of it and disappear.

The following morning, I got in early with the express intention of calling the police, but found a grim-faced wing PO waiting outside my office. He said Rocky was insisting on seeing me and he was in a very agitated state, claiming his life was being threatened.

Rocky told me he'd been confronted the previous afternoon by the officer who'd confessed to killing his wife. He'd accused Rocky of informing on him. He said he'd denied it, but he was sure the PO didn't believe him. I immediately had Rocky transferred to a single cell in the seg unit for his own protection. I had no doubt that the PO would soon work out it was connected to what he'd told Rocky.

Less than five minutes after Rocky had left my office, the PO turned up and demanded to see me. Once inside my office, he immediately announced that he had something 'very important' to get off his chest.

"I know he's told you I killed my wife, right?" he said.

I nodded.

"It was just a wind-up, guv," he said, laughing out loud. "It's complete bollocks but he took me literally."

He also insisted that Rocky was obsessed with the subject because of what he'd done to his own wife. The PO said he believed Rocky was using the entire story to try and get his own sentence reduced. But Rocky hadn't actually asked for this.

When I pointed this out to the officer, he grimaced and said in a manic voice that Rocky was pulling the wool over my eyes. Then he sprung to his feet and left my office without saying another word.

I immediately tracked down one of the police officers who'd worked on the original missing wife enquiry. He surprised me by admitting that he'd always suspected the wife might have been murdered by her husband. As there was never any proof, though, the investigation had to be dropped.

* * *

That same afternoon, I sat in on an interview between Rocky and two homicide detectives in my office. They asked him to recall everything he'd told me the previous day. To my disbelief, he said he didn't know what they were talking about. One of the police officers tried a gentler approach, talking sympathetically about the murder of Rocky's own wife. This didn't work either, and Rocky still refused to talk about any of it.

The other detective stepped in, trying to pressurise Rocky, who reacted by demanding to be returned to his cell. I told Rocky that I realised he was scared but he needed to tell the police everything he'd told me. He shook his head, stood up and again demanded to be taken back to his cell.

After he'd gone, the two detectives seemed very irritated. One said he felt his time had been wasted by coming to the prison in the first place and inferred that Rocky had probably made up the entire story to get a lighter sentence.

I had no doubt the PO had intimidated Rocky to stop him talking to us, so I suggested to the detectives that they came back the following day to interview Rocky a second time, because he might hopefully be more cooperative after a sleepless night in his cell. Unfortunately, Rocky refused to meet the detectives again the following morning and told staff on the seg unit that he didn't want to leave his cell because he was scared someone might hurt him. He refused to say who that person might be.

That afternoon, the PO was walking casually down the corridor towards Rocky's cell in the seg unit when me and three officers asked him to accompany us to my office. When he was searched, a knife was found hidden in one of his boots.

The two detectives who'd earlier interviewed Rocky were waiting for the PO in my office. They produced CCTV footage which clearly showed the PO knocking on the front door of a house with a bunch of flowers in his hand and a woman answering. The footage had arrived at the prison in an anonymous envelope that morning and the house featured in it was Rocky's family home.

The PO was trying to intimidate Rocky into not giving evidence against him by visiting his second wife. Rocky had discovered all this during a phone call the previous day to his wife. She'd mentioned that a man had turned up with a bunch of flowers. Rocky knew from her description that it had to be the PO plus he had security cameras at the front of his house which filmed his visit.

Back in my office, the PO looked stunned when he was shown the footage. There was only one conclusion, which was that he was trying to cover up the murder of his wife after all. After the detectives had played the footage back to him a second time, the PO shrugged his shoulders and said he might as well get everything off his chest. It was time to tell them the truth at last.

Within 20 minutes, he'd made a full confession about killing his wife. The following day, he led detectives to his wife's remains buried in a wood near the family home. A post mortem revealed she'd been beaten to death.

The PO eventually pleaded guilty to murder and was sentenced to a minimum of 20 years in prison. Rocky's role was never mentioned in open court because the police felt that his own conviction might be used by the PO's defence counsel to cast some doubt on the prosecution's case.

Rocky never asked for anything in return for his help bringing that PO to justice, but I informed the parole board about what he'd done and he was granted a two-year reduction to his original 15-year sentence for killing his wife.

Just before Rocky was released from prison, he wrote me a letter wishing me well and promising he'd never be coming back to prison ever again. He also told me that bringing that officer to justice had helped him come to terms with his own offence and all the destruction it had caused his family.

The last I heard of him was that he and his new wife were running a small hotel on the south coast of England.

CHAPTER 35
DESPERATION

Many people who know very little about prison are always surprised by the number of female inmates who gain a lot of weight while incarcerated. I guess they assume there can't be enough food there for this to happen. I've come across some who've ended up putting on as much as five or six stone in a year in prison.

A lot of female inmates blame depression and boredom for causing these weight problems. In a mentally challenging environment like prison, perhaps it's not so surprising that food becomes a vice for a lot of extremely vulnerable women inmates. None of this is helped by the attitude of some hard-nosed old POs such as one I worked alongside who said this about obesity in prisons: "You feed 'em up and slow 'em down. It makes my job much easier when they're too tired and fat to fight back at me and the system."

The problem of obesity as well as other serious mental health issues was why I considered family days such an essential 'tool' for improving inmates' psychological welfare inside all the women's prisons where I served as a governor.

At one of those prisons, I encountered a female prisoner with three children under the age of five, who was a classic example. Her children were being looked after by her mother. This particular inmate had been imprisoned on relatively minor drug charges but had suffered continual mental health problems during her incarceration because she missed her kids so much. Her weight had ballooned and most of the staff felt very sorry for her. This inmate insisted she'd always been a good mother on the outside. The POs believed her because whenever her children came on one-hour visits, they were always well behaved and seemed genuinely happy to see her.

During the build-up to this inmate's first family day, she became terrified of doing anything that might prevent her spending a whole day with her kids – and that resulted in her putting on even more weight through excessive over-eating. Staff reported that she was a nervous wreck most of the time and they were worried about her mobility because of her obesity.

All around her were other inmates whose criminal lifestyles had ended up costing them their families, who now wouldn't be coming for family day. Some of them became extremely bitter and jealous as the day approached because it excluded them. A couple of these inmates had already made life quite difficult for the mother of three and she'd been unfairly labelled as a bit of a snob, as some inmates believed she looked down her nose at them when in fact she was just extremely shy, especially because of her weight.

More than a week before family day, one of the inmates approached this mother of three in the yard and told her she'd just heard from the main wing PO that she wasn't going to be allowed to see her family because her excess weight made her a health risk. It was nothing more than a spiteful wind-up, intended to screw with the mother's head, but, unfortunately, it worked. She lost it and dragged the other woman to a quiet corner of the yard and tried to beat her up.

The PO who broke up the fight said afterwards she felt genuinely sorry for that mother of three because she knew how much she'd been looking forward to seeing her children, and now we would have to restrict those privileges. When she pleaded for a second chance, the PO told her that the governor was the only one who could make that decision, but I was away at a conference that day, so unable to make the meeting the mother requested.

Later in the yard, she bumped into the inmate who'd wound her up. More words were exchanged and the mother of three said later that at the time her head was spinning with anger. All her dreams of seeing her beloved children seemed to have disappeared into thin air.

When she got back to her cell and her cellmate asked her if she was okay, she flipped out, produced a knife she kept for protection and took her cellmate hostage just after they had been locked down. When a PO walked past the door a few minutes later, she screamed out that unless staff got hold of me to come and speak to her, she would kill her cellmate.

After being informed of this in a phone call, I headed straight to the prison to talk to her, saddened to hear what had happened as I knew how much her children meant to her. In the corridor near her locked cell door, staff informed me she'd been saying over and over again that she had nothing to live for if she couldn't spend the day with her kids.

I spoke to her through the cell door and emphasised to her that she would have been allowed to see her children on family day if she hadn't got into trouble. But taking a hostage meant there was now no way I could reverse that decision. It felt risky to tell her that, but I had to be honest. She didn't respond, so I retreated to give her time to think through her situation.

Neither my staff nor I wanted to storm the cell, unless it was absolutely essential. We couldn't be sure that the cellmate was safe and wanted to make sure she would be okay, so I put the National Tactical Response Group (NTRG) on alert to be prepared to move in. As I approached her cell again, I heard her talking to the cellmate she was holding hostage.

"I'm so sorry, luv," she told the woman. "You don't deserve any of this."

Then she yelled through the door: "But I don't know what else to fuckin' do."

I poked open the flap in the cell door and noticed she was grasping the knife in her hand very tightly, as if she was getting ready to use it. So I turned and signalled with my hand to the POs to prepare to force entry into the cell. Glancing back through the flap, I could see she was now holding the knife at the throat of the other inmate.

"Sorry," she said, looking straight at me.

With my hand behind my back, I beckoned the unit to move in as fast as possible. Back inside the cell, she took the knife away from the cellmate's throat and pressed the pointed end of the blade into her own wrist, just above the palm of her hand.

As we burst into the cell, she ripped a line through the skin of her swollen arm all the way up to the inside of her elbow before dropping the knife on the floor. Blood gushed out of the open wound as she collapsed and lost consciousness. I snatched the knife off the floor in a pool of her blood as the POs helped the cellmate out of the cell. She seemed more worried about the mother's injuries than her own predicament.

"Please help her," the cellmate said to me, as the POs led her out. "She only wanted to see her kids. I know she'd never have hurt me."

The following morning, I met a group of inmates from the wing who pleaded with me to allow that inmate to see her family, despite what had happened. I told them that, much as I would want to grant that wish, the prison service was adamant it could not happen. They pointed out that if she snatched anyone during the family day and someone was hurt, we'd be liable for it all. I rang the inmate's mother to break the news to her. I heard two of her children crying in the background after she told them the news while she was talking to me on the phone.

Family day went ahead a week later for all the other inmates as planned, though. Towards the end of the afternoon,

I visited the POs' office that overlooked the reception area. A few minutes later, that mother's three children and their grandmother entered the office alongside two POs.

Then, down below, the mother was escorted by two officers to a standing position close to the office window that overlooked the wing reception area so she could be seen clearly. She smiled and waved up at her mother and her children, and they waved back.

It wasn't nearly as good as family day but at least she got to see them for a few minutes, albeit through a glass window. The kidnap charges against that inmate were eventually reduced to minor disciplinary matters after her cellmate said she didn't want to give evidence against her.

The mother of three was eventually released from prison on condition she agreed to have a full mental health evaluation. A few months after her departure, she came back into the prison as a volunteer helping women inmates cope with their weight problems. She'd lost three stone and told her old wing governor she would never lose her children ever again.

The cruel irony of prisons is that sometimes they can provide the spark that lights something up in a positive way.

CHAPTER 36
PLAYING THE SYSTEM

One of my most important jobs as a governor was to try and restrict the activities of the most manipulative inmates in order to maintain peace and order. It was a lot harder to do this, though, when I found myself dealing with a new inmate who'd once been a prison officer and so knew exactly how the system worked.

This ex-PO had been found guilty of perjury after providing a false alibi for a gangster he'd first met in jail, which almost got that crime boss off murder charges. During the crooked officer's trial, he'd been branded a sociopath, who was said by prosecutors to manipulate everyone around him.

All the staff had been warned about this inmate days before he arrived. My prison had been deliberately chosen by the authorities because it was hundreds of miles from where he'd worked as a PO, so he wouldn't be able to take advantage of any local connections. I warned the staff not to take notice of the media stories about this ex-PO because it was imperative we began on a clean slate with him, whatever we felt about his crimes.

Within 48 hours of arriving in a sweat box at the prison reception area, he'd been fully processed and taken to the wing. We'd assumed he'd suffer at the hands of other inmates, just like most incarcerated POs and police officers do. But staff reported that he'd immediately begun strutting around the wing like some kind of hard man.

Then he surprised many of us by introducing himself to everyone on the wing and openly referring to his own offence. After that, the ex-PO 'got to work' recruiting weaker inmates to do all his dirty work for him.

One of the ways in which he exerted power was by helping them construct legal defence letters to use in appeals against their sentences, which so many try to do inside prison. And of course, he'd seen it work enough times to know how to offer effective advice.

Next he set up a card school with a group of older prisoners, knowing full well it blatantly defied prison rules. While betting isn't allowed, I ordered the staff to ignore the rules for the moment, as I didn't want a confrontation with the ex-PO so early on. If his actions were meant to goad us into responding, I knew that would have played right into his hands.

The general wing population soon began commenting to staff about how unsettling this ex-PO was, though. One told an officer: "He's got most of us in the palm of his hand. Nobody dares cross him. The fact he's a screw makes him even scarier because he doesn't act like one."

Once he'd recruited his own crew of tame prisoners, the ex-PO then turned his attention to me. I was touring the wing when he approached me in the exercise yard and asked bluntly if I had a problem with him because he was a former PO.

I knew he was deliberately confronting me to impress other inmates who were watching us, so I ignored his question and asked him very politely how he was settling in. And at that very moment, it dawned on me that the best way to handle him was to divert him away from his power-playing games on the wing.

I told him to report to me the following morning because I wanted him to work as a clerk in my office. He seemed completely thrown by my job offer and just mumbled, "Thanks," before walking away. My primary motivation for this was to remove him from the wing for six hours every day and hopefully water down any criminal activities he might be tempted to get involved with.

I even made a point of not engaging much with him when he first began working in my office, unless it was absolutely necessary. I didn't want him to feel too comfortable and I needed to ensure he didn't think he was in control of me. And to his credit, this ex-PO inmate threw himself into the job with great energy and enthusiasm and I was careful to avoid talking to him about his double-dealing crimes. That wasn't my job anyway.

A few weeks after he'd started working in my office, however, the staff reported that he'd become much more frosty towards them back on the wing. I presumed he was probably doing this to keep the professional villains and other inmates on his side. I'd heard from staff that they'd become increasingly suspicious of him since he got that job in my office.

Despite that day job, he'd got involved in a number of low-level criminal activities, including money lending, selling tobacco and offering needy inmates protection. POs reported that, while he was happy getting involved in pretty much anything else, he carefully avoided anything connected to drugs on the wing. He told one wing officer that he disapproved of narcotics completely.

I wondered if this negative attitude towards drugs would eventually lead to problems with other inmates, as narcotics fuel so many aspects of life in prisons, especially the male ones. In my office, though, his behaviour continued to be exemplary. I gradually gave him extra responsibilities, knowing full well it would most likely create a bigger gap between him and other inmates on his wing, who continued to be suspicious about our relationship.

Eventually, I even allowed him to accompany me to law enforcement meetings in different parts of the UK as an assistant. It was my way of telling both the staff and inmates that I trusted him, to a certain degree at least.

Out on the road, the ex-PO became something of a mini-celebrity. A lot of people inside the prison service were intrigued by how he'd ended up being my 'assistant'. On the wing, some inmates remained bemused by him, while others thought he might be trying to ensure he kept a 'clean sheet' so that his parole application would be quickly approved when he got near to the end of his sentence.

Around this time, a number of younger inmates arrived on the wing and soon made it clear they were planning to take over the wing's drug business from the older prisoners running it. None of this suited the ex-PO. Not only was he fiercely anti-drugs but he also didn't like the way the younger inmates were trying to muscle in on the wing's other established criminal activities. This bitterness culminated in a ferocious argument in the canteen between the ex-PO and two of the new inmates, which had to be broken up by four officers.

The following day the ex-PO complained to me when he was working in my office that the younger inmates were blatantly selling drugs on the corridor near his cell.

I warned him that this might provoke problems for him with those younger inmates, but he said he didn't care because ultimately he just hated drugs. So, I ordered wing POs to launch a crackdown on the drug-dealing on the wing.

A few days later, two of those younger inmates cornered the ex-PO in the showers and gave him what they referred to as 'a little present' by taking it in turns to slash their shivs across both his cheeks. After spending two days in a hospital, the ex-PO returned to the wing insisting he didn't want to be put in the seg unit for his protection. Officers reported that he was never quite the same after that attack, though. My wing staff also advised me not to rehire him to work in my office because they were very worried there would be more recriminations from those younger inmates if they thought he was still close to me.

After that, the ex-PO rarely left his cell and handed over all his prison 'businesses' to the inmates who'd attacked him. And he never once tried to stop them selling drugs on the corridor near his cell. The ex-PO had been extremely arrogant and ignored the classic warning that inmates should never forget: namely that in prison, no matter who you are, there's always someone around the corner waiting to take you on.

* * *

That ex-PO had discovered the hard way that prison is never easy for anyone.

I came across one ex-policeman in prison for corruption who actually seemed to genuinely want to keep a low profile, although he discovered to his cost that was a lot easier said than done. He'd ended up in prison after being trapped in a web of vice and drugs by a gang of professional criminals. They'd blackmailed him into giving them information from the police's national computer database.

He told me following his arrival at the prison where I was governor that he was relieved he'd been caught because he was convinced he'd either have died from an overdose of cocaine or the gangsters would have killed him. Inside prison, he carefully avoided all narcotics and insisted that all he wanted to do was get through his sentence in one piece. He seemed contrite and said he dreamed about returning to the real world and leading a normal life with his family after his release.

Some of the prison's more old-fashioned professional criminals tried to intimidate this corrupt cop when he first arrived on the wing. Then another inmate, a British drug lord with a lot of power, stepped in and warned them all to leave him alone. It turned out that the corrupt cop had arrested the drug lord once in the past but allowed all his family to go free on humanitarian grounds. Hence, he had a lot of respect for the crooked policeman, or at least owed him a debt of gratitude.

This protection didn't stop some of the other inmates speculating that the corrupt cop was an undercover police plant spying on them. The drug lord insisted this wasn't the case, but, with rumours already flying around the wing, the ex-detective began receiving death threats.

When I heard from staff what was happening, I offered him a transfer to another smaller prison. But he turned down my suggestion because he wanted to remain as close as possible to his family home, so his wife and children could visit him regularly. Unfortunately, this only meant the hate campaign against him continued. One time he found broken splinters of glass in his food in the canteen and on another occasion, an inmate threatened to knife his wife during a visit.

A lot of the staff were perplexed as they'd thought the ex-cop was being protected by the drug lord. Then I began to get reports from senior staff that there were rumours circulating the wing that the ex-cop had begun snorting cocaine again. Apparently, he'd also got into a few nasty altercations with some of the inmates, who were still accusing him of being an undercover cop, and clearly the cocaine was his escape from the terror.

When I asked the senior wing POs to look into what was going on, they reported back that the aggressive inmates were being paid by the same drug lord to intimidate the ex-cop because the ex-cop had refused to help him facilitate the payment of a bribe to a serving police officer that he knew.

In layman's terms: the ex-cop 'owed' that drug lord and it was payback time.

I eventually hauled the ex-cop into my office and asked him what on earth was going on. He just shrugged his shoulders and said: "Listen, guv, I got everything I deserved for being a bent copper. If someone wants to give me a hard time in here, there's nothing I can do about it. As long as I get through this in one piece I don't really care."

Back on the wing, the ex-cop continued suffering on all levels and I got further reports he was consuming even more booze and drugs. When his wife and children arrived at the prison for a visit, POs had to tell them they couldn't see him because he was so intoxicated he couldn't leave his cell. When staff disclosed all this to him the following day, he burst into tears. He'd been so high that he'd completely forgotten they were coming to see him.

A few weeks later, the ex-cop was found collapsed in his cell. He'd had a drugs overdose that had brought on a heart attack. He survived, although seemed to become a much harder, more distant character when he returned to the prison from hospital. He eventually requested that move to the smaller jail that I'd first offered him many months earlier. When I asked him why he'd changed his mind, he said his wife was divorcing him and there was no point being near to his family anymore because they'd refused to see him since that time when he was too high to see them.

My deputy governor later told me he'd heard that after the ex-cop eventually got out of prison, he went to work as a henchman for a gang of professional criminals. There were rumours he helped kill some of the gang's enemies before then himself disappearing.

The tragedy of prison is that often even those who genuinely intend going straight can find themselves trapped in a corner with no choice but to reoffend.

To me, this is yet more evidence that the rehabilitation system needs to be drastically overhauled. But despite all my good intentions, I still hadn't come up with anything that could actually help to improve that aspect of the prison system.

CHAPTER 37
CHILLING

Back in the late 1980s and early 1990s, when I first started out in the prison service, you could tell who the powerful criminals were simply from the way they walked and talked. They handled prison as if it was part of their job, a job they were good at. While I was a governor, though, a different, younger breed of gangster boss began appearing in prisons, and they tended to be a lot more varied and much less predictable.

One example of this was a drug baron whose Christian name sounded more like someone from a Jane Austen novel than a member of a ruthless cartel. He even spoke with an upper-class-sounding public school accent when he was talking to prison staff, although his voice would drop to street level when he was communicating with the general prison population. He also didn't have a single tattoo, which made him even more unique inside prison.

This inmate had the threat of more jail time hanging over him unless he paid back the £4 million that the police had estimated as his income over the previous three years while operating as a drug baron. But he made it clear from the first day he arrived on the wing that he had no intention of paying back a penny of those alleged earnings. In fact, his way of dealing with this issue was to completely deny he'd ever been in the drug business in the first place.

At his earlier trial, the police alleged he was an extremely dangerous character capable of hurting anyone who got in his way. They also claimed that he'd had a number of his underworld enemies killed, though they'd never found enough evidence to prove it in a court of law. Yet inside prison, he appeared a much more measured character than most inmates. He chose his words carefully and you could see his mind running through all his options before he responded to any question you asked.

He watched his back at all times, well aware that anything he said might be used against him by police, who were determined to nail him for those alleged murders and expose his hidden narco fortune. Many inmates tried to befriend him from the moment he arrived on the wing. My staff reported that he'd been very wary of them all at first, while he worked out whom to trust.

He eventually recruited three henchmen to accompany him whenever he was out of his cell. He also managed to swap his 30-a-day smoker cellmate for another prisoner after producing a doctor's note via his lawyer, claiming he suffered from an allergic reaction to cigarette smoke.

I'd initially intended to turn down his request because the prison wasn't obliged to provide a comfortable environment for inmates. They were there to be punished for breaking the law, after all. But the police asked me not to object because they wanted to lull him into thinking he had power and influence on the wing. They hoped he'd then do something which would help them build a new case against him.

During a visit to the wing, I casually reminded this young inmate that I'd done him a big favour by changing his smoking cellmate. He seemed thrown by my laid-back tone but still managed to give a measured response.

"That's a given, sir," he said, using the posher version of his voice. "I just want a quiet life here. I don't plan to stay a second longer than I have to."

His wing actually went through a very quiet period over the following few weeks. Senior POs believed it was down to this young drug baron warning all the main troublemakers on the wing that they'd be 'dealt with' if they caused any problems for the staff or inmates. And most weeks, a procession of expensive lawyers visited the drug baron as he continued fighting his legal battle against the police's confiscation order for the return of that £4 million in profits from his narcotics business.

He boasted to one PO on the wing that all the police claims would soon be dropped because there was no concrete evidence that the money even existed. The police had no intention of giving up that easily, though. I'd heard from one friend inside the police that they had a new informant who'd told them about two offshore bank accounts connected to the young baron, which they believed contained more than double the $4 million they were chasing.

The young drug baron eventually heard about this during one of those meetings with his lawyers. He was so outraged he turned a table over, smashed two chairs up and his lawyers had to press the alarm bell for assistance, after which they informed their client they were no longer prepared to represent him. The lawyers were eventually rescued from the interview room by three prison officers, who then shackled the young drug lord and escorted him back to his cell.

Over the following couple of days, officers on the wing reported that the baron was being extremely aggressive towards staff. He almost started a riot after one PO ordered him to speed up a phone call because so many inmates were queuing up behind him.

A few days after this, two men submitted applications to the prison administration office for permission to visit him. Neither of them had ever been in to see him before. Their names were cross-checked on the prison computer and it turned out they both had criminal records.

I informed the police about their applications to visit. They were so suspicious they suggested the pair might be planning to help the drug lord escape. But there was no tangible evidence this was really going to happen, so I took the decision to show some compassion and allow the visit and hope it would go off without incident. It was a big risk. But as my very able deputy governor reminded me, if I started refusing visits by convicted criminals, then a lot of prisoners would end up with no one coming in to see them.

Visiting inmates at most prisons is always a slow process. Visitors are usually advised to turn up at least an hour before the time that visits are due to start. This gives staff ample time to search each person entering the prison and check their credentials. My deputy and I plus a couple of senior POs decided to watch the visitor car park and prison entrance that morning on the jail's CCTV system from the control room, just in case something happened.

The car park soon filled up with at least 20 vehicles containing visitors, who then headed towards the entrance to the main reception area. From there they'd be going through the swing gates, to where they'd be thoroughly searched before being allowed further into the prison. The majority of those gathered in the car park that day were women and children visiting their loved ones. There was no sign of the two men, who'd been issued prison passes earlier that week to visit the young drug lord.

Most visitors had already moved through to the main reception area when a white two-door Mercedes Coupé swept into the car park. Two men in their mid-twenties got out of it and immediately began walking across the car park towards the entrance to the prison reception area. Two young Muslim mothers in burkas with children were the only others still waiting to go through the swing gates. Me and my three colleagues remained glued to the CCTV monitor in the control room as the two men who'd arrived in the Mercedes continued walking towards that same entrance.

One of the Muslim women at the back of the queue suddenly turned around and began heading back towards the parked cars as if she'd forgotten something. As she passed the drug lord's two visitors going the other way, she pulled something out from under her abaya and turned towards them. It was a sawn-off shotgun and 'she' held it like gangsters in Hollywood films usually do: a tight grip around the trigger and the palm clasped the forearm. To me, that gave the game away as to 'her' identity; I could tell it was a disguise.

One of the POs next to me in the control room hit the alarm and the other officer screamed into his walkie-talkie as I watched the 'woman' in the burka aim the weapon at the head of one of those two men and squeeze the trigger twice in fast succession.

'Her' target fell to the ground instantly. The other man turned and ran back towards the Mercedes. The man in the burka calmly got into a Ford Fiesta and drove off moments before three POs appeared in the car park from the main prison building. The Mercedes followed out of the gate seconds later. Two of the POs ran to the shot man and knelt down beside him. One of them tried to resuscitate him. But it was already too late.

The audacity of that hit in the prison car park was breathtaking. Whoever had commissioned the killing must have been sending out a message because the target had been one of that young drug lord's closest associates. The entire prison was immediately locked down on my orders, just in case the shooting had been some kind of diversion to enable the baron to escape.

When I visited him in his cell half an hour later with my deputy governor, he shrugged his shoulders and said, "That's a shame," after I told him about the shooting of his friend. My deputy governor pointed out afterwards that the young drug lord's reaction seemed shockingly indifferent, considering the victim was supposed to have been one of his best friends. Life was clearly very cheap to him.

It wasn't until a week later that the same detective I knew admitted that the victim had been their secret informant, who'd been helping them track the young baron's earnings from the drug trade. I was infuriated that the police hadn't told me this before.

The same detective even admitted that the victim had been advised by them not to cancel the prison visit in case it made him look as if he had something to hide. They said they didn't want to risk their informant's life by telling me, but they'd ended up doing exactly that because the baron already knew that one of his men visiting that day had been helping the police nail him.

Clearly, no one thought the drug lord would have the audacity to have that man killed in the grounds of the prison where he was locked up. But having met him, I have to say I wasn't that surprised. The police eventually abandoned their investigation into that shooting, the murders of at least three other gangsters and those offshore bank accounts, as all the baron's associates were now too scared to help them. The killing in the prison car park had worked well from his perspective.

Back in prison, the drug lord once again turned into a model prisoner and, after the police had dropped all their enquiries, instructed his lawyers to sue them for harassment.

He was eventually awarded more than a quarter of a million pounds in compensation.

Following his eventual release from prison, I heard he went on to become an even richer and more powerful criminal. That young gang boss had turned out to be even more shrewd and power-hungry than the old-school professionals who came before him.

I admitted to my deputy at the time that there had been moments while dealing with him when I started to question my effectiveness as a prison governor. The cold-blooded mentality driving on that ambitious gangster had led to him ordering a hit *inside* my prison grounds. And afterwards, he'd even proved himself to be powerful and wealthy enough to literally get away with murder.

This brand new generation of professional criminals was more than likely going to make my job as prison governor even harder.

CHAPTER 38
LOST IN SPACE

That killing in the prison car park got me thinking seriously about where my career was going. Maybe it would be better if I did get out while I was still on top. My deputy governor was an excellent officer and he deserved to take over the reins.

But while I considered my future, I came across one inmate who presented probably the most unique challenge of my entire career. He was a cybercriminal who perfectly represented the detached reality of crime in the twenty-first century. This offender had been sentenced to five years in prison for using an online role-playing game to nurture a teenager with mental disabilities into carrying out a shooting spree at his school.

Fortunately, the cyber manipulator got cold feet at the last moment and anonymously tipped off the police about what was about to happen. The teenage shooter himself was arrested and told police about the internet game and how the characters in it had 'persuaded' him to launch an attack. A police cyber expert eventually tracked the communications from the game on the teenager's computer back to this older man and he was arrested.

Prison was a massive wake-up call for the cyber manipulator when he arrived. He didn't seem able to cope with not being allowed a laptop or a phone, and staff repeatedly found him wandering around the corridors looking lost and seemingly too afraid to talk to any other inmates. It soon became obvious that he'd been so indoctrinated by the internet and social media that he was unable to properly interact with anyone in the real, offline world.

POs reported that he spent much of his time in his cell meditating. On the rare occasions when he actually made it out to the yard, he'd sit cross-legged on the ground in a corner, chanting. His family background didn't help, either. He was the son of a pharmaceutical corporation chairman and had been brought up in a huge, detached mansion in the Home Counties. His mother and father had disowned him after his arrest in the shooting spree case.

His family wealth made him a classic target on the wing and a number of inmates tried to extort money from him by offering him protection in exchange for a weekly 'fee'. When one wing bully attacked him in the showers, he threw himself to the floor, curled up in a ball and withstood a severe kicking without making a sound. After it was over, he got up, dusted himself down and walked straight back to his cell without saying a word to anyone.

When one of the POs later checked in his cell to see if he was all right, he found him on the top bunk bed, sitting cross-legged and chanting until his cellmate walked in and told him to shut the fuck up. In the canteen, the computer nerd usually ate on his own in a far corner away from all the other prisoners. When one group of younger inmates sat down next to him and tried to intimidate him, he didn't even look up at them. In the end, they just gave up and walked away.

Staff concluded that he must have smuggled some drugs into the prison because he was so spaced out the whole time. When a raid was carried out by POs on his cell, he calmly stood by and watched the entire search with an expression of complete detachment. One of the officers searching his room asked him if he'd been taking drugs and he simply shook his head. They found nothing in his cell. I ordered my wing staff to provide regular reports on this inmate. It sounded as if he was on the verge of some kind of nervous breakdown, and there was always a danger this could lead to violence.

One senior wing PO unofficially took him under his wing and suggested to me that he should be given the prison job of office computer maintenance man. This meant he'd be responsible for ensuring all the machines in the prison management offices were functioning to their full capacity.

Some senior staff were worried he might start using the computers to communicate with people outside the prison, so I made sure my staff were close to him at all times when he was in the offices.

Occasionally, I'd sit down with him and the office manager at the end of a work shift for a cup of tea and a chat. Initially, he barely spoke a word, but I was determined to try and bring him out of his shell. We started with basic conversation about the weather, but when I switched to football we quickly reached a dead end. He had no interest in sports, but my deputy governor and I turned him into a challenging work project. We knew that unless he came out of his cyberworld shell, then he'd really suffer inside prison.

This inmate was perceptive enough to know precisely why we were trying to help him become more of a normal person. It took almost six months to turn him into a fully functioning member of the prison population. He learned how to make conversation, stopped avoiding other inmates and even started to be on reasonably friendly terms with many of the wing staff. This new-found social interaction also helped him to come to terms with his offence. He opened up to us about his rich and toxic parents, explaining that his lonely childhood drove him to turn to the internet for friendship.

After his eventual release from prison, this inmate opened a computer software security firm that was rapidly swallowed up by one of the world's biggest online software manufacturers. I read an interview with him in a magazine just after that and he said that if it hadn't been for going to prison, he would never have escaped the darkened room at his family home where he'd lie on his bed trying to dream up ways to manipulate teenagers into committing murder.

So sometimes prison really can make a difference. But despite this, I didn't feel as connected to my job as I once had been. I'd always promised myself I'd jump before I was pushed and maybe now was the time for that decision?

CHAPTER 39
BREAKING THE BARRIER

As a prison governor, I always tried to operate an 'open door' policy when it came to both my staff and inmates. I wanted them to come to me with all their problems because I was convinced that if they felt someone was always prepared to listen, then it would make everything a little easier to sort out. But not even I could have predicted one of the problems that came my way just days after I'd decided to retire from the prison service.

It all started with a request for a meeting from one of my senior wing POs. He was a solid, quietly spoken character known for his patience when dealing with the inmates under his care. However, on this occasion, he was anxious to discuss one of his younger staff members.

"There's something wrong with him," he told me, within seconds of sitting down for our meeting.

"What do you mean, exactly?" I asked, trying not to sound too dismissive, despite the vagueness of what he'd just said.

"Well, there's the nail varnish to start with," explained the PO. "Then the other day he came in wearing eyeliner."

This young male PO had been wearing make-up to work and it had not gone unnoticed by staff and inmates. The senior PO explained that he'd asked the young officer why he was wearing it. He'd then apologised profusely and said he was a goth and had been to a couple of music concerts the previous weekends and forgotten to remove it all.

I shrugged after he told me this as it didn't seem such a big deal. I'd been quite closely involved with the recruitment of this young PO myself, after concluding he'd be an interesting addition to the staff. He was a former psychology student and had worked in the theatre before deciding to join the prison service. I could tell from the expression on the senior wing PO's face that he wanted to tell me more, so I urged him to continue.

He explained that although this young officer was over six feet tall and should have been more than capable from a physical standpoint, he was incredibly timid with inmates and had also failed to properly engage with his colleagues on basic work duties. The senior PO said it was clear his mind wasn't on the job and he was worried that the young officer might be having some kind of breakdown. I couldn't take any direct action based on what little he'd just told me, so I asked him to keep an eye on him and see how everything panned out.

Three days later, the same senior wing PO waved me down as I was about to get on my motorbike in the prison staff car park. He was out of breath and seemed very anxious. He said he'd just had a call from a hospital saying the same young officer had been admitted after trying to commit suicide at his home.

The PO suggested that I should accompany him to the hospital to see him. Since I'd always prided myself on being hands on, I agreed. The young officer looked extremely worried when we both turned up at his hospital bedside. I said I was only there to see if I could help him in any way. I also tried to reassure him that his job was safe and that he should take off as long as he wanted before returning to work.

He seemed relieved, but then lowered his voice and asked if the senior wing PO could wait outside because he had something important to discuss with me. I nodded at the officer, who seemed relieved to leave us to it and said he'd head off home rather than hang around for me.

After he'd gone, this young officer told me he had a lot of 'stuff to sort out', although when I tried to get him to expand on what he meant, he clammed up. The conversation then became peppered with long, awkward silences. I was about to get up and leave when a middle-aged woman walked in with a bunch of flowers and announced she was his mother.

As I stood up to introduce myself, I noticed her glance at her son nervously. Given the obvious tension in the room, I said goodbye and headed out into the ward's corridor. Moments later, I was waiting by the hospital lift when the mother appeared alongside me and explained that her son was very shy and worried that he might lose his job. Anxiously looking around, she lowered her voice and then told me that he wanted to have gender transition surgery. He'd actually worn the make-up and nail varnish to work as a 'test' to see how his colleagues and inmates reacted.

After she'd finished, I urged her to take me back to his bedside. There, I explained to him that we'd have to 'manage' his situation very carefully, otherwise it would disrupt the wing and maybe even put the staff and inmates' security at risk. He nodded in agreement, surprised by my helpful attitude. I said I'd arrange for him to speak to the wing supervisor before he returned to work, as it was important he felt he could be open about his situation to his colleagues on the wing.

I also informed him that prison rules at that time did not permit inmates or staff to have gender transition operations. I did assure him, however, that I'd try my hardest to get the policy reversed so he could have surgery. I did warn him that he would have to continue working until that came through. I knew he wanted to hold on to his job, so I asked him to be patient because all this wasn't going to happen overnight. I didn't tell him I was about to hand my notice in to my prison service bosses, though.

My decision to quit actually seemed to energise my efforts on his behalf, because I no longer had a career to fret about. And I had no intention of leaving this issue as unfinished business for my deputy to have to deal with, or anyone else who took over as governor.

The following morning, I met up with the senior wing PO who'd come to see me in the first place and explained everything to him. He seemed surprised I was being so relaxed about it. We agreed that this young officer should work nights, so he'd be less exposed to the inmates.

After he'd departed, my deputy assured me he'd back me to the hilt, even though I knew he had to watch his step because he was hoping to become a fully fledged governor himself after my departure. Since I already had a meeting scheduled with the service's top administrators to announce my retirement, I decided to inform them of this young officer's predicament at the same time.

One administrator even asked me if my decision to quit was in any way connected to what he described as my 'radical opinions' about the young officer. I took a deep breath and ignored the insinuation that I was in some way being disloyal to the service. In fairness to the two others on that panel, they listened carefully to my argument in favour of allowing this young officer to have transitional surgery, and this all conveniently helped water down any attempt by them to try and dissuade me from retiring. At the end of the meeting, they promised they'd make an official decision as quickly as possible regarding the transitional surgery, but that it would take some weeks.

Back inside the prison, despite trying to keep it under wraps, it didn't take long for the rumours about that young officer to start circulating throughout the prison.

The day after he'd returned to work, he phoned me in tears after facing a barrage of homophobic and transphobic insults from inmates, who were shouting at him from behind their locked cell doors while he was patrolling the wing at night. He pleaded to be allowed to take some time off so he could have the transitional surgery. Unfortunately, I had to insist he continued working until the operation was officially sanctioned by the prison service, otherwise he would lose his job.

I began to think that maybe he should leave the service. His presence on the wing was provoking so many problems, for both him and us, so perhaps it would have been easier for everyone involved. However, that would have been a climb-down after I'd made so much effort to help him and I didn't want to cause him any more stress in case it sparked another suicide attempt. So instead I suggested he switched back to day duty where we could all keep a closer eye on him.

A few days later, he was on duty in the yard when there was a clash between a group of Black inmates and a gang of right-wing skinheads who were taunting them with racist insults. Despite a tirade of homophobic abuse from the skin-heads, the young officer ordered them back to a far corner of the yard before carefully ensuring that all the Black inmates could safely return to their cells. Not only were the other staff members impressed but the Black inmates made a point of thanking him for the way he'd handled such a potentially dangerous situation.

That incident was a turning point for this young officer. By managing to hold his head up high and ignore the insults, he'd shown he could rise above it all. Eventually, staff and inmates began openly engaging him about his plans to change sex and I went back to the prison service to press them for permission for him to have his surgery.

Something must have clicked with them in the end because less than a month later, the young officer was given special dispensation from the prison service to go ahead with the transitional surgery. Just three weeks after the operation, he returned to the prison with a new Christian name and full make-up. Staff members and most inmates greeted him like a long-lost old friend.

However, that young officer had been through an unnecessarily harsh process thanks to the prison service system and this left me realising that, despite my success in helping him, I'd made the right decision quitting the prison service. Three decades after I'd started, there still remained inside the prison service a large core of individuals prepared to fight against 'radical' staff like me.

After years battling to improve conditions and change some of the old-fashioned rules and regulations, it also felt as if I'd lost touch with the real reasons why I'd entered the prison service in the first place. At least knowing I was leaving now lifted some of the weight of all that responsibility off my shoulders, though.

I even began looking around for new challenges still connected to prisons but a long way from the lethargy of the UK system. I was convinced that prisons in other nations could be the answer because they'd surely be more open to change?

It was time to open a new chapter in my life.

EPILOGUE
LIFE BEYOND THE BRIDGE

I was filled with a myriad of emotions when I got to my last day as governor inside the UK prison service. I'd chosen to leave a financially secure position to go and work in the real world far beyond the gates of any prison. At least I had a new job to go to, though, unlike most inmates I'd encountered over the previous 30 years who had left the four walls of their prison without so much hope.

On that last day, I turned my attention towards one particular prisoner who was due out at the same time as me and whom I'd spent some time talking to over the previous few weeks. I knew only too well that the POs would enjoy keeping him hanging around in the reception area that day right up to the last moment before finally letting him out. The way they did that summed up how much inmates were disrespected and how the officers held power over them for as long as they were inside.

The world that inmate was about to re-enter was not going to be easy to survive in either, especially on just £100 a week unemployment benefit. I already knew from speaking with him that he just wanted to get out as quickly as possible and return to his family. In that respect, he was one of the lucky ones because he still had a family to go home to.

Imagine for a moment what it must be like to be released from prison after a long sentence. Everything is alien to you. Two-way roads have turned one-way. Entire towns have transformed from what you knew. Family members have grown and changed. That inmate had even told me that he'd been particularly dreading how his teenage daughter would react to him when he got out. When I asked him why, he'd said he hadn't allowed her to ever visit him in prison during his five-year sentence, after telling her in a letter that prisons were dangerous places full of dangerous men.

"So now she thinks I'm one of those bad men," he explained.

No wonder he was full of so much trepidation about the outside world. I just hoped this inmate's confidence wouldn't plummet once he found himself facing up to so much unrecognisable adversity. A lot of prisoners have told me down the years that they call this feeling 'life beyond the bridge' because many of them really do live in fear of crossing that bridge back to the so-called real world. In some ways, I felt exactly the same way about my future.

Back in the reception area on my final day, the prison staff looked at me as if I was completely bonkers when I told them I was going to walk out of the prison alongside that inmate, so they'd have to let him out earlier than they'd intended. Less than an hour later, we headed past the POs in the reception area and the inmate even managed to crack a few friendly jokes with a couple of them.

Once outside, we walked along a walkway enclosed with high chain-mesh fencing towards the swing gates to the main prison exit. I noticed a woman and two children standing about 30 yards ahead of us, looking anxiously in our direction. When the inmate next to me saw them, he waved frantically and said goodbye politely before running the final 15 yards into their arms. Then he turned and looked back towards me and shouted: "Thanks for everything, guv."

I watched all four continue hugging as they walked towards the visitor car park. It was a timely reminder of what I missed about my own family. Then I turned to take in one last look at the prison I'd once ruled. It looked so austere and uninviting that I was relieved to finally be leaving the rain and concrete behind.

That building summed up the often substandard world we expect prisoners to live in. Prison conditions provoke more riots and general disharmony than anything else. Inmates need to feel they're being treated like human beings, whatever they've been convicted of doing.

I was leaving behind the same old fundamental problems inside the UK justice system. Overcrowded prisons. Inefficient and impersonal rehabilitation systems doomed to failure. Poorly paid staff, often disconnected from the inmates they're supposed to protect.

As I walked away from that prison, if felt as if I'd failed after decades of good intention.

ENDNOTES

DRUGS

Many jails across the UK were built between 100 and 200 years ago, so it's hardly surprising they're in a poor state of disrepair. However, by forcing inmates to live in squalid, substandard conditions they quickly lose their self-esteem and this has undoubtedly led to the explosion in drug use inside UK prisons in recent years. As a governor, I often felt genuinely ashamed that the service had failed so comprehensively to stamp out the vast consumption of narcotics within prisons.

Today, many drug dealers in the UK's biggest cities boast that they can make bigger profits getting their product into prisons than selling it out on the streets. One gram of cocaine that costs a maximum of £100 out on the streets can fetch as much as £500 inside prison. Cannabis prices are said to often quadruple for customers behind bars.

Then there is the synthetic drug spice, a lethal cannabis substitute. More prisoners have consumed spice than any other drug over the past decade. Since the Covid pandemic, I'm told that the more traditional narcotics such as weed, speed and cocaine have also made a big comeback in prisons, which all goes to show how easy it is to smuggle any drugs inside.

This drugs epidemic inside UK prisons relies on a sophisticated network of criminals, whose job is solely to supply narcotics to jails. There are even prisoners using secret mobile phones inside their cells to set up these deals. There is also usually a middle man – often known as 'the networker' – who purchases the narcotics on the outside and then gives the drugs to a mule, who hides them in their body before entering a prison. And then there are those convicted drug dealers already incarcerated in UK's prisons who sell these narcotics to other prisoners.

One inmate once told me: "Prison is actually a better place to sell drugs because no one will inform on you and there is a 500 per cent mark-up on them when they get into a jail."

I've known of some inmates who became heroin addicts *inside* prison after never having touched any drugs while they were outside in the so-called real world. I've also come across inmates who are so worried that their drug habits will worsen in prison that they refuse to see any visitors in case narcotics are passed on to them. Outside some UK prisons, drugs are being openly flown into cells on drones operated by drug dealers standing just outside the jail perimeter.

There's one particular urban prison I've visited in recent years where you can hear the omnipresent insect-style buzz of drones flying in and out of the cell windows most late afternoons. Many POs on the ground are extremely resentful about the drugs explosion inside UK prisons. They believe they should be paid extra danger money for having to deal with volatile inmates high on drugs. And the comprehensive drug treatment programmes available for any inmate caught taking drugs inside UK prisons seem to have made little difference as so few attend them.

THE PANDEMIC

The Covid pandemic caused much of the world to shut down in early 2020. It's still ongoing, as I write this book, in the late summer of 2021. Spare a thought for the staff and inmates during this health crisis because both have suffered enormously, especially when it comes to mental health issues. Officers on the ground have had an appalling time, especially at the start of the pandemic when fear and trepidation ruled and it was predicted that prisons would become rampant Covid hotspots.

There were also fears that prison staff would panic and threaten to go on strike if they felt the authorities were not providing enough protective equipment for officers, so governors and managers weren't given an easy time of it. It was even rumoured that some inmates might try to infect their least favourite POs with the virus and that having Covid could give them some power they never previously had.

But instead of jails becoming unruly during the pandemic, there was actually less violence and the service believe this was down to the way that inmates embraced rather than rejected the strict new rules that had to be introduced to cope with the threat of Covid. This entailed clampdowns on movement and social interaction, and often it meant inmates being in their cells for much longer periods than pre-pandemic.

Prison visits were also heavily restricted, especially during the first UK lockdown in spring 2020. Many had gloomily presumed this would also spark problems inside this country's prisons. But it never happened.

One recently retired PO told me: "We expected everything to kick off when the first full lockdown came into force but, on the contrary, prisons got quieter and easier to work in. Many inmates really suffered. The threat of Covid was constant and they couldn't even see their loved ones. It's truly remarkable that there were so few problems."

As another PO I know explained: "Most inmates acted very responsibly. They saw what was happening on the TV news and accepted that the lockdown had to go ahead. They didn't fight it. In a weird kind of way, we all embraced it together. It felt as if the staff and inmates were actually on the same side for once. That helped lift the morale of the prison where I work and I heard it was the same across the country."

The only disturbing consequence of the pandemic inside prisons was that some Chinese inmates found themselves under threat because their home country was being blamed for starting the pandemic in the first place. I was told that in some prisons, Chinese prisoners were put in the seg wing for their own protection.

The way that staff and inmates responded to the pandemic serves as a reminder to normal, law-abiding citizens that prisons are not all full of hardened criminals who do not care what society thinks about them. The way the entire UK prison service coped with Covid should be applauded.

SMOKING

For many decades, the prison authorities unofficially encouraged smoking inside all prisons in the belief that it helped calm down many inmates and any attempt to restrict it would lead to major discipline problems inside prisons across the country. Then back in 2007, the UK prison service announced a ban on smoking in all enclosed spaces within prisons. In all honesty, this was never fully enforced as there would have been uproar in jails across the nation.

Today inmates are encouraged to vape within the confines of their own cells and a lot of smokers continue to ignore the so-called ban on actual cigarettes when they're out on their wing. Prison officers themselves tend to avoid reprimanding inmates for smoking on the basis that there are far more important issues that need to be dealt with inside prisons.

As a result of all this, even some of the newest prisons in this country smell smoky and stale. Non-smoking inmates are not supposed to have to share cells with those who do smoke anymore. But that decision rests with the staff on each wing, and if there is overcrowding, then it's often ignored.

The prison service offers inmates who do smoke a facility to attend classes to try and stop smoking, although it's rarely taken up. Thus, this entire issue continues to be side-stepped by the UK prison service, which conveniently ignores the plight of POs who inhale all this smoke without any consideration for their long-term health.

At the time of writing, it seems unlikely that the smoking 'debate' will be properly settled any time soon.

REALITY CHECK

UK government cuts over the past decade are threatening to decimate this country's prisons. Even former chief inspector of prisons Lord Ramsbottom has recently called for a public inquiry into why so much money has been cut from the prisons budget. He accused politicians of leaving prisons "hugely understaffed" and POs' pay is so low that it's attracting fewer and fewer new recruits. No wonder another staffing crisis looms on the horizon.

Why would anyone want to spend up to 12 hours a day in a prison for a starting salary of £24,700?

As the prison service faces even further expenditure cuts, many believe that the increasingly squalid and dangerous conditions behind bars can only get worse and this has no doubt contributed to the increase in violent attacks on UK prison staff in recent years.

Back in 2016, around 10,000 officers walked out on strike after new figures revealed there had been 23,000 prison assaults over the previous year, including 6,000 attacks on staff and a 38 per cent rise in violence involving weapons. The UK Ministry of Justice's own data shows assaults on prison staff in England and Wales have increased overall by 247 per cent over the past decade.

Back in the autumn of 2016, rioting inmates overran Bedford prison, just a few weeks after two inmates escaped from London's HMP Pentonville following a spate of stabbings, one of which involved the killing of an inmate with a hunting knife.

As a result, the then justice secretary Liz Truss announced a £550 million plan to tackle the crisis, pledging to hire 2,500 more officers, revamp ageing jails, and install sophisticated 'jamming equipment' to block the use of mobile phones inside prison. The Ministry of Justice also promised a 'new strategy for tackling corruption' inside prisons.

But by the middle of 2021 most of these measures had not materialised and the UK's prisons remained dangerous, volatile places where death and injury are commonplace.

REHABILITATION AND TREATING MENTAL ILLNESSES

Rehabilitation is one of the most emotive phrases inside the prison service. Some believe it's the key to reducing the UK's prison population, while others complain it provides criminals with often meaningless help after their release from prison. I'm convinced it's the most important route out of the problem of overcrowded prisons in this country.

A lot of inmates I've encountered after serving time in prison have turned their lives around, thanks to skill training for professions in everything from cookery to accounting. There are also educational and behavioural courses which have been around inside prisons for decades. And today there is a new cluster of other initiatives available to help inmates readjust to society following their release.

Courses also include something called 'Restorative Justice' which is specifically designed to enable prisoners to acknowledge the damage they've caused to themselves and others through their law-breaking. Inmates are even encouraged to meet victims of crime, although not those who were affected by their own offences.

In recent years residential treatment centres have been opened throughout the UK as alternatives to prisons for offenders with mental health problems. These days, this is called 'secure care'. Such inmates often suffer extreme guilt for their criminal actions which can spark a wide range of illnesses including schizophrenia, psychosis, acute depression and bipolar disorder. Incidents of self-harm are also highest among this group of inmates.

Many of these new residential treatment centres are converted mental hospitals, carefully re-equipped to handle this new type of resident from regular prisons. The centres are classified as a security level below better-known mental institutions such as Broadmoor, Ashworth and Rampton, which are England's three best-known top-security psychiatric hospitals, often described as prisons because they're surrounded by high walls and sealed entrances.

Unlike in normal prisons, smoking is entirely banned in these residential treatment centres and residents are encouraged to use on-site gyms and sports halls. Inmates are even allowed the use of a computer. This has helped many prisoners adjust more to what they can expect on their release from their sentence.

I visited one of these new centres shortly before I quit the UK prison service. It was located in the heart of a typical Middle England village and contained 30 bedrooms for its residents. No one is ever referred to as an inmate or prisoner here.

Inside it I met former criminals who claimed to have discovered a new lease of life by being given proper mental health treatment, which gave them hope they had a future in society on their release from prison. One man told me he had no doubt he would have ended up offending again on his release if he'd been kept in a regular prison, because of his obvious mental health problems.

Another resident I met was a diagnosed schizophrenic, whose life had revolved around substance abuse and crime since he'd left school. After two years in one of these centres, he'd been allowed to go into the local towns unaccompanied. After keeping out of trouble, the date for his release from his original sentence was brought forward as a reward for his good behaviour. If he'd still been in a normal prison, he would have been released into society with no proper support system, nowhere to live and would probably have soon started reoffending.

It's important to clearly state that none of this comes cheap. It's estimated that each resident in one of these centres costs £150,000 a year, nearly five times as much as a male inmate in a category B prison. There are now 50-plus similar institutions set up throughout England and Wales.

There were none when I first started out in the prison service, so at least we're moving in the right direction.

BEREAVEMENT

In the late spring of 2021, screenwriter Jimmy McGovern's prison drama *Time* was screened on BBC TV to great acclaim. It was deservedly hailed as one of the most accurate and moving series about prisons ever televised.

One issue it focused on was the main character's desperate attempt to be at his own father's funeral. In a heartbreaking sequence, we watch that character – played by actor Sean Bean – about to be given compassionate day release to go to the funeral. But it's then revoked, so he misses the funeral and hits rock bottom. In real life, I have to say it's much the same.

As a PO and governor, I always tried to be sensitive to inmates' needs when they suffered a bereavement because I'd long been appalled at how little was done for prisoners going through such emotional turmoil. Imagine how they feel. It must be a horrible combination of guilt and loss, to have not been there in their loved ones' final moments and never again be able to see them. It is without doubt one of the greatest hardships of all for inmates.

Today, there are a number of special licences that can be applied for so an inmate can visit a dying relative or attend a funeral. They come with multiple caveats, though, which makes it easier to refuse such permissions than grant them. There is always a fear in the back of the mind of prison staff that the inmate in question might abscond when he is out on release – and then the staff who gave him or her permission in the first place would be blamed.

The other option is for an inmate to apply to be escorted to a funeral by a minimum of two POs. But that's such a humiliating process that most prisoners prefer not to go at all because they don't want to put their families through the embarrassment of uniformed guards being present at a funeral.

Inmates who suffer a bereavement are also supposed to be offered pastoral care from the prison chaplain, although they have to apply for it and prisoners are rarely willing to do that. It's one of my biggest regrets that I was never able to introduce new guidelines that might enable prisoners not to suffer so extensively after a bereavement.

FRAILTY

The plight of elderly inmates is a serious ongoing problem, with the UK prison population getting older and older. This was perfectly illustrated by one of London's most legendary gangsters, who arrived at a prison where I was governor a couple of years before I retired.

By this time he was in his mid-seventies, although still allegedly very active in the UK underworld. He'd begun his 'career' as a henchman for one of London's most deadly crime families back in the early 1960s. Then he'd graduated to bank robberies followed by the narcotics underworld when recreational drugs, especially cocaine, took off in the early 1980s.

His most recent arrest had come during a police sting operation after he'd paid £5 million for a shipment of cocaine being supplied directly to him in London by a cartel in Colombia. Unfortunately for him, the South Americans who dispatched the drugs to him suspected he was an agent for America's Drug Enforcement Administration (DEA) and so the UK police were told the cocaine shipment was heading this way. He ended up with a 12-year stretch. Despite his age, within days of arriving on the wing he was caught up in a vicious fight in the yard and stabbed in the arm. He ended up having treatment in the health unit of the prison.

On the second day of his stay in that unit, I got a message from one of my senior wing officers that he was asking for a meeting with me. Later that same afternoon, he visited my office and profusely apologised for being involved in the knife fight and insisted he didn't know what had come over him. He asked me if I could arrange for a medical assessment to be made of him because he felt 'something wasn't right' in his head.

Two days later a prison service doctor informed me that this inmate was in the early stages of Alzheimer's. When I revealed this to him, he said his main priority was to prevent other prisoners finding out because it would seriously damage his credibility inside and outside of prison.

He also asked me if he could be transferred to the seg unit because he felt he'd be safer on his own. Once on the seg wing, he paid for his own television and a constant supply of books to read and over the following six months, his Alzheimer's appeared to be manageable.

Then one morning, a PO entered his cell to tell him his breakfast pack was still outside his door. He looked up blankly and said: "Who are you? Where am I?" When his wife and adult children came in to visit him that afternoon, he didn't even recognise them. Following another examination by the prison doctor, he was then moved on compassionate grounds to a secure nursing home in the Home Counties.

It's important that people outside the prison service appreciate just how many of the problems inside prison are really no different from what happens in the outside world. He was one of the lucky ones. It's reckoned that today there are thousands of inmates still inside jails across the UK suffering from geriatric health problems.

FEMALE STAFF

It might surprise many to discover that women have served as prison officers in the UK since the early nineteenth century. Today they make up about 30 per cent of all the officers working inside male and female prisons in the UK. I'm a great supporter of them because they undoubtedly help prisons to be calmer places than they used to be.

The realisation of this by the service has also led to women prison governors being appointed. But it hasn't been an easy ride for any of them. They've had to battle blatant sexism, which still to this day includes a dismissive attitude towards their professional abilities.

Some years back, one of the UK's toughest prisons appointed a female governor, despite the opposition of the majority of staff at that jail. The prison had a reputation as one of the most corrupt in the country and many staff believed that a woman had been appointed governor because she was thought to be a lot more trustworthy than any of the male candidates for the job.

This particular governor had been fast-tracked through the UK's prison services promotion system, which was designed to enable people with relatively little on-the-floor experience of prisons to enter at a low management level, rather than starting as a prison officer. She was a former medic whose only involvement with prisons had come through jail visits and working at a training centre for prison officers. However, many staff inside the prison believed that whoever ran their jail should come from a 'proper prison background', as well as being locally connected.

Three weeks after this governor took over the prison, a full-scale riot almost erupted when a group of angry inmates mounted a noisy protest against prison conditions. The new governor initially ordered POs not to use any force. The prisoners had expected to fight the staff but when no one went near them, they didn't know what to do. Then the new governor strolled on to the wing and insisted on talking directly to the ring leaders of the protesting inmates. They were so impressed by the respectful and fearless way she treated them that they backed down immediately.

Over the following six months, this female governor changed the entire ethos of the prison. Violent incidents dropped by a quarter week on week. Drug-dependency incidents were cut by a third and POs themselves reported a significant 'sea change' in the relationship between staff and inmates.

However, there remained a handful of dinosaur POs who insisted that all these improvements just happened to coincide with the appointment of the governor. They even sneered at the new governor's decision to visit all the prison wings every weekday to assure staff and inmates she was always available to discuss all their problems.

She also introduced new classes for inmates, including everything from computer science to masonry. Two football pitches were laid out in the prison grounds for inmates and staff, as well as a mini-golf area. Yet the old-school staff members continued mocking her behind her back. Many of them had started at the prison back in the days when it was condemned by inspectors as being 'inhospitable, squalid and unstable' for staff and inmates.

Today it's been transformed into a model prison reputed to be one of the best-run jails in the world. And much of that is down to their new female governor.

HOME TERRITORY

Throughout my career, I always tried to show compassion towards the families of inmates. They go through a lot of heartache and turmoil because of something they weren't responsible for in the first place.

Having a close relative in prison is devastating for those on the outside and many relatives have approached me down the years with prisoner transfer requests because they wanted their loved ones to be in a prison as near to where they lived as possible.

But imprisoning inmates close to their old 'territories' can often be a problem because they can more easily continue running their illicit activities from a prison cell near to home. This in turn also helps encourage gang-related activities in that area to continue.

There were and still are a small handful of regions in the UK where professional criminals seem to have almost as much power as the police. And prisons in these areas have huge problems controlling their inmates for that very same reason. I worked as a PO in one which had an explosive atmosphere virtually round the clock, with staff constantly struggling to retain control of the wings.

That prison seemed to be run with a completely different set of rules to what I was used to. There was a disturbing familiarity between staff and inmates, many of whom had grown up in the same community where this prison was located.

This community familiarity is particularly problematic at a women's prison where I worked. A couple of years before I arrived, local inmates and prison staff joined forces to run a brothel close to that prison.

The male PO involved had recruited female inmates shortly before the end of their sentences and persuaded them to work as prostitutes because they were all short of money and lived in the vicinity. If that prison had not housed local inmates, then the crooked PO probably would not have been able to recruit those women in the first place.

THE STONE AGE

Even as I write this book in the early autumn of 2021, the vast majority of UK prison officers do not regularly wear bodycams or carry walkie-talkies. That is shocking in this high-tech day and age, especially since both items are essential to the work. In many other countries, they are used as clear deterrents.

UK prison authorities insist the service simply doesn't have the funds to pay for every officer to have such equipment. Even some of the inmates are outraged about this because many of them believe that bodycams would help expose officer brutality towards them.

POs in modern Britain do, however, continue to wear a white shirt, black tie, black trousers and black boots. They also have what is known as a 'woolly-pully' jumper and/or a black soft shell fleece jacket.

Stab vests and other protective gear are only worn when they need to take such precautions, including during the transportation of inmates from one prison to another or to and from court for a hearing.

It seems ironic that those two pieces of 'kit' that really could help save lives are still not given any priority in this day and age.

THE UNITED STATES OF CRIME

In the US, the majority of prisons I visited were run with racial lines at the core. At no prison I went to did I see that real effort had been made to properly integrate races of prisoners.

Men's penitentiaries in the US certainly lead the world when it comes to humiliating inmates. They're forced to wear leg chains whenever they're moved anywhere and the majority of staff treat them with such coldness and detachment that it no doubt contributes to an even worse atmosphere between the staff and inmates.

The end result is that many male inmates in US jails are violent, resentful and hell-bent on revenge against staff, as well as against society in general. Many leave jail convinced their only chance of survival is to commit more crimes. And this American prison system clearly hasn't worked because the US has the highest per capita prison population in the world and its jails remain overcrowded concrete jungles to this day.

In the UK, we do like to think we're a more liberal society but I noticed, as many others have, that the prison service has been gradually adopting more of an American mentality in recent years. A lot of this is down to pressure from politicians, who think they can attract votes by pushing for a no-tolerance attitude when it comes to criminals, an attitude I'm proud I didn't adopt in my time.

AFTERMATH

I was convinced I wouldn't miss any aspect of working in the UK prison service after my roller-coaster ride of more than three decades.

A few months after I left, I started work at what I'd presumed would be a fairly relaxed, relatively small prison on a paradise holiday island thousands of miles from the gritty, grey corridors and walls of the UK prison service.

I quickly discovered that those expectations were utterly naive and unrealistic. A lot was very similar, but the biggest difference from back in the UK was that all the prison staff including me, the new governor, had to carry a gun at all times.

This undoubtedly contributed towards a tense climate of fear throughout this prison. I soon became aware of the staff beating inmates on a regular basis, and the suicide rate was five times more than what it was back in the UK.

I'd thought I would be coasting through the rest of my professional life and then in the evenings writing this book on a sandy beach with a cocktail in one hand and the sun setting in the distance over the ocean. Instead, I quickly began missing the UK and the comradeship, and sometimes even the inmates, I left behind.

Today, I'm hoping to return to the UK soon and I hope that I might at least find a part-time executive post in a prison. On the other hand, I might not be deemed suitable in the eyes of the new, financially obsessed prison service.

But I still feel I have so much to offer.

CONCLUSION

So that's my strange selection of carefully camouflaged prison tales. There are loads more I could have written about but they can all be saved for another time.

The main thing, from my perspective, was that my recollections reflected the complex nature of life and death inside prisons. My intention was never to shock and upset people but to show that jails are a lot different from how they're so often portrayed.

I also hope that some people who've read this book might feel inspired enough to consider a career in the prison service. We need a diverse range of staff to effectively guard prisoners more than ever before. This diversity will hopefully bring about a gradual rethink when it comes to the way prisons are run, although there are still many hurdles to jump.

The biggest sea change of all is to convince the public that prisons are not just about punishing people. We need to give offenders a chance in the big, wide world, whatever life has thrown at them.

The prison system must recognise and nurture inmates so they can appreciate there is hope for them. That means making sure they're fairly treated rather than dumped on life's scrapheap.

At the end of the day, I still fear there are many people inside the UK prison service who think that we should just throw away the key and let the supposedly bad people of this world rot in our jails.

We as a society can't afford to just keep filling up prisons to bursting point. This will cripple the finances of this country and be rightly seen as an admission that the system has given up on people.

I've tried here to tell a balanced and fair account of my experiences in the UK prison service, despite changing the names, places and details to protect the innocent (and the maybe not so innocent).

I work in one of the only businesses in the world that wants fewer customers, and I have always kept that in mind.

FINALLY – MY SECRET

They say prisons are full of deep and dark secrets. I've carefully protected my own biggest secret until now because I wanted the story of my prison service experiences to be untainted by my own personal choices.

Writing this book has forced me to deal with many aspects of my life, so now seems the right time to lay it all out.

My secret is something that most people would have virtually always kept to themselves until very recently. But in today's modern society, it's not such a life-shattering revelation, so it's definitely time to get it off my back.

My true sexuality first dawned on me during the painful weeks and months before and after the break-up of my marriage almost 20 years ago.

Today, there is a new spirit of tolerance and understanding in UK society, so being gay and running a prison really is no big deal. It's one of my biggest regrets that I didn't come out much sooner.

I just sincerely hope there isn't a staff member at any prison where I've worked who'd claim that my sexuality impeded my abilities as governor and prison officer. I'm also convinced that if I was coming out now as a serving prison governor or PO, inmates and staff would have respected me for being upfront about my sexuality.

For that reason, I want to urge and encourage all gay inmates and prison staff to be as open as they feel comfortable when it comes to their sexuality, because it will most likely help them to live a much more fulfilling life.

ACKNOWLEDGEMENTS

I'd like to express my gratitude to the worlds of law enforcement and crime. I'm not able to identify most of these people in public for reasons already explained. But their lives and experiences have contributed greatly to this book. Many thanks to you all.

Blessed are the peacemakers, for they shall be
called the children of God.

MATTHEW 5:9

A tattoo belonging to the finest PO
I ever worked with, the Prison Singer.